Sharing God's Love and Joy

52 DEVOTIONAL BIBLE STUDIES FOR SENIOR ADULTS

Willa Ruth Garlow

WestBow
PRESS
A DIVISION OF THOMAS NELSON

WestBow Press books may be ordered through booksellers or by contacting:

WestBow Press
A Division of Thomas Nelson
1663 Liberty Drive
Bloomington, IN 47403
www.westbowpress.com
1-(866) 928-1240

Because of the dynamic nature of the Internet, any web addresses or links contained in this book may have changed since publication and may no longer be valid. The views expressed in this work are solely those of the author and do not necessarily reflect the views of the publisher, and the publisher hereby disclaims any responsibility for them.

Any people depicted in stock imagery provided by Thinkstock are models, and such images are being used for illustrative purposes only.

Certain stock imagery © Thinkstock.

ISBN: 978-1-4497-1671-4 (sc)
ISBN: 978-1-4497-1672-1 (e)

Library of Congress Control Number: 2011928532

Printed in the United States of America

WestBow Press rev. date: 05/20/2011

CONTENTS

SUGGESTIONS FOR SUCCESSFUL DEVOTIONAL TIMES WITH SENIOR ADULTS

1. Ahead of time, make definite plans for each of the devotional times for which you are responsible.

2. Before the seniors arrive, gather the materials and supplies needed for each devotional time.*

3. Arrange the room so that everyone can see and hear.

4. Avoid making the seniors sit and wait for a long time.

5. Keep the devotional times short, no more than 20 to 30 minutes from start to finish.

6. Make the devotional times interesting, happy, and relevant to the lives of seniors.

7. As much as possible, involve the seniors in the devotional times

8. In each devotional time, intermingle songs, speaking, and activities.

9. Use songs familiar to seniors.** If possible, provide accompaniment such as a piano or guitar.

10. Remember that seniors enjoy singing songs that they know, enjoy hearing their group singing even when they don't participate, and enjoy hearing special music by singers and instrumentalists. Seniors love to hear children sing.

11. So that devotional times are not always the same, vary the schedules and activities.

12. Always be loving and respectful to every senior adult attending the devotional times.

13. As much as possible, anticipate and try to avoid being distracted by interruptions that may occur during devotional times with seniors.

14. Each of these suggested devotional times includes a suggestion for an optional, simple craft. If a craft is provided, assemble the supplies have them ready to use.

* This book provides four devotional time suggestions for each month. On pages 123–124 are four additional devotional time outlines for use when a month has an extra devotional each quarter.

** In this book's devotional time suggestions, most of the suggested songs are from:

Sonshine Songs and Scriptures, Victory Edition, The Sonshine Society, P.O. Box 327, Lynnwood, WA 98046-0327

FOREWORD

Bill Pierce

The joy to be found in the discovery of God's word is a lifelong journey that can begin at any age. This book is full of Bible studies that have been written specifically for use by people who have experienced life for a few years and their families. Willa Ruth Garlow is a gifted Bible teacher and writer. I first began attending the conferences she led when I was in college. She has the wonderful gift of illustrating God's Word and applying it to our lives. She has a love for God and for people that comes alive in these 52 studies – one for every week of the year. If you lead a weekly Bible study for older adults, you will find this rich resource very helpful and rewarding. These lessons can be used as a weekly or monthly study in churches, retirement communities and many other settings. They also make a wonderful devotional Bible study at home. You will be blessed. May God bless the study of His Word.

PREFACE

My prayer is that these devotional-time suggestions will be a blessing to senior adults, senior care staff and the persons who present and participate in these devotions.

Thank you to Chris Finley, director of chaplain services for Baptist Village Communities of Oklahoma (BVC). He saw a need and envisioned a devotional times book for senior adults. He and Dr. Bill Pierce, BVC president, honored me by allowing me to put together these devotional guides.

Thanks to all of you who, through the years, have taught and inspired me in sermons, Bible studies, seminars, books, other printed materials and conversations. From these I gleaned and jotted down ideas for some of this book's materials.

My personal gratitude goes to my husband, Dr. J. Lyle Garlow, my parents (now deceased), Dr. Sam and Naomi Scantlan, our daughter, Dawnellen and son, Sam. They have been and are a source of love, joy and inspiration to me.

Many versions of scripture are used, including King James, New International, New American Standard and the Living Bible, among others.

God bless all of you who use any part of this book,

Willa Ruth Garlow

Happy New Year!

Suggested materials: Bibles, songbooks, and New Year's horns and other noisemakers

Devotional Time Suggestions

- Begin by wishing everyone a happy New Year and giving them a New Year noisemaker or rhythm instrument.

- Ask participants to keep time with their noisemakers while the group sings "Auld Lang Syne" and "Happy New Year to you, God bless you this year" Tune: "Happy Birthday to You."

- Read Psalm 96:1–4a and Philippians 4:4.

- Prayer thanking God for the New Year.

- Song: "In My Heart There Rings a Melody" to celebrate God's goodness and the joy of the New Year.

It's January! Happy New Year

January is a time for us to stop and focus on the brand new year that God has given us – a *new* start – a clean slate. The old year is gone. We can thank God for His blessings in the past, but we can look forward to, with God's help, starting a new future, a new beginning in this new year which the Lord has given us.

1. We have a new year, but God gives us a precious gift that is not new.

   God gives us His love. Ask the group to quote John 3:16. God made you. God made you special. God loves you, and you can count on God's love.

   Read (or ask someone to read) Romans 5:8 and Romans 8:35–39.

   God sent His Son to redeem us and to save us from the eternal punishment of our sins. No one can separate us from God's love! His love is not new this New Year.

2. We have a new year, but God gives us another precious gift that is not new.

God gives us His grace – His unmerited favor. We can count on God's love, but we can also count on His goodness to us.

Read (or ask someone to read) Philippians 1:2.

God's grace and goodness give us reason to rejoice. God's grace gives us hope for this New Year and hope for eternity.

3. We have a new year, but God gives us yet another precious gift that is not new.

God gives us His help, comfort and peace – no matter what the circumstances.

Read (or ask someone to read) Psalm 32:4, Isaiah 51:3, Isaiah 66:13.

Jesus promised us that His Father, God, would send us the Holy Spirit to comfort us and give us personal peace.

Read John 16:7, 13, 31–33.

How good God is! Because of His love and grace, we can have comfort and peace.

- Song/chorus, "God Is So Good" (three times)
    - First time: "God is so good, He gives us love."
    - Second time: "God is so good, He gives us grace."
    - Third time: "God is so good, He gives us comfort and peace."

- Pray again, thanking God for a new year, but also for His love, grace and comfort that are not new and are available to each of us.

- Fun song (use the noisemakers to keep time with the music): "We wish you a happy New Year, happy New Year all year!" Tune: "We Wish You a Merry Christmas".

If you choose to provide a craft, make New Year's bookmarks.

Supplies:
- Heavy, colored paper, cut into bookmark shapes
- Message strips with the words, "Happy New Year. God loves you!" typed on sheets of white copy paper
- Scissors
- Glue
- Hole punch
- Ribbon (quarter-inch wide)

Give each person a bookmark shape and a "Happy New Year" message strip. Allow each person to cut out the typed message and glue it on a bookmark. Punch a hole in the top of each bookmark and tie a ribbon through the hole. Write each person's name on the back of his or her bookmark.

Jesus and the Cross

Suggested materials: songbooks, two sets of large letters (C-R-O-S-S cut out of construction paper), poster board, tape, a cross necklace or bracelet and a small rugged cross made from sticks or scrap lumber

Devotional Time Suggestions

- Begin with singing "Near the Cross."

- Prayer thanking God for Jesus and the cross.

- Song: "Jesus Paid It All"

- Read about the crucifixion of Jesus (John 19:15–18).

- Song: "At the Cross"

- Prayer thanking God for salvation and for Jesus bearing the cross for our sins.

The Cross

The cross is more than a pendant on a necklace, chain, or bracelet. (Show a cross necklace or bracelet)

The cross is more than crude pieces of wood tied together. (Show a cross made of two pieces of wood)

The dictionary defines a cross as an upright post with a bar across the top on which ancient Romans fastened convicted persons to die.

The songs that we have just sung are songs about the cross of Christ, God's perfect Son, who willingly gave His life on the cross for us.

Let's look at some letters and words that remind us how much God loves us. As you talk about each of the five letters, lightly tape (or ask someone to tape) the letter to the poster board.

C – is for *Christ*, God's Son. Christ was sent to earth and endured death on the Cross because God "so loved the world."

S – is for *saves*. Christ saves us from our sins and gives us eternal life. He came to earth for one reason. Read Matthew 18:11.

R – is for *redeems*. By God's grace and mercy, when we accept Jesus as our personal Savior, we receive salvation and eternal life. Read John 3:17.

S – is for *showing*/proving God's love for us by sending His Son to die for us.

O – is for *overcame*. On the cross, Jesus overcame sin, death and the grave. He overcame the power of Satan and proved He is powerful enough to save us and give us life eternal with Him. Read 1 Corinthians 1:18.

As you make these final statements, put the letters in order to spell *cross*.

These letters represent our salvation, our acceptance of Jesus Christ as our personal Savior:

> **C** – is for Christ.
> **R** – is for redeems us.
> **O** – is for overcame our sins.
> **S** – is for saves us from our sins.
> **S** – is for showing God's love.

- Special music (solo): "The Old Rugged Cross"

  Ask the group to sing along on the chorus.

- Prayer thanking God for sending His Son, Jesus, to die on the cross to save us from our sins.

If you choose to provide a craft, make a cross wall hanging.

Supplies:

- Sheets of colored construction paper
- Half-sheets of coordinating colors of construction paper
- Cross shapes cut from white construction paper
- Glue
- Glitter
- Hole punch
- Ribbon (quarter-inch wide)

Glue glitter on the cross shapes. Glue the cross shapes in the center of the construction paper half-sheets. Next, glue the half-sheets in the center of the whole sheets. Punch a hole in the top of the whole sheet and tie a ribbon through the hole to make a wall hanging.

God's Eye is on the Sparrow

Suggested materials: Bibles, a display of bird figurines and bird pictures, the suggested scripture passages written on paper strips (if you plan to assign different people to read the passages), the music and words to the song, "His Eye Is on the Sparrow"

Devotional Time Suggestions

- Begin by saying that in this time together, we will talk about and look at Bible passages about birds in God's world.

  When God created the world, Genesis 1:21–22 reports that "God created every winged fowl after his kind: and God saw that was good. And God blessed them saying let fowl multiply in the earth."

- Ask the group to name different kinds of birds:

- Mention that God made some birds with bright colors, and some with drab colors that blend with the natural background.

  When a little girl saw a brightly multicolored macaw, she said, "Didn't God do good?"

- Ask participants, "Have any of you ever had a pet bird?" Allow time for several individuals to tell about birds they have owned or seen.

- Special music (solo or duet): "His Eye is on the Sparrow"

  On the last chorus, ask the entire group to sing along, "God's eye is on the sparrow, and I know He watches me."

- Scripture reading: Matthew 10:29–31: God cares and watches over you and me.

- Repeat singing the chorus, "God's eye is on the sparrow, and I know He watches me."

- Scripture reading: Psalm 104:16–17

  God provides for the birds and He provides for us.

- Repeat singing the chorus, "God's eye is on the sparrow and I know He cares for me."

- Scripture reading: Song of Solomon 2:11–13a, God makes the seasons for us to enjoy.

- Repeat singing the chorus, "God's eye is on the sparrow and I know He cares for me."

- Scripture reading: Luke 12:6–7

  Luke and Matthew both recorded Jesus talking about birds; they remind us that God knows you and me, will not forget us, and will be with us.

- God made us a wonderful, beautiful world in which to live and enjoy. God loves you and me.

- Pray, thanking God for His promises, for His love and care, for watching over us.

- Let's leave with a song in our hearts. Sing the chorus one more time: "God's eye is on the sparrow and I know He cares for me."

If you choose to include a craft, paint small plaster-of-paris bird figures.

Supplies:
- Simple, small bird figures (available at hobby stores)
- Acrylic paints
- Paint brushes
- Small bowls of water for cleaning brushes
- Clear plastic spray for finishing the birds when the paint has dried

The Bible – Wonderful Words of Life

Suggested materials: songbooks and several Bibles of different sizes, colors and translations for display

Devotional Time Suggestions

- Song: "I Love to Tell the Story"

- Pray, thanking God for the Bible and its message to us.

- Song: "Tell Me the Story of Jesus"

The Bible

- Show and talk about the different Bibles on display. No matter the size, color or translation, the message remains the same.

- When you were younger, do you remember someone to whom the Bible was special? Was there a man or woman who helped you begin to understand and love the Bible? (Allow time for answers)

- A song that young children sing at church is, "The Bible is a special book; I like to hear its stories." The Bible *is* a special book.

- Why is the Bible special?

  - The Bible is special because it is God's Word to us. The Bible was written by men who were inspired by God. Read 2 Timothy 3:16. The Bible – God's Word – is true. Read Psalm 119:160, and then verse 152.

  - The Bible is special because it gives us guidance and direction for our lives. Read Psalm 119:11–16. God's Word must be an important part of our daily lives. Read Psalm 119:105.

  - The Bible is special because we find comfort in its message. The Bible gives comfort and hope even in sadness and pain. Read Psalm 119:49–50. The

Bible helps us find peace. Read Psalm 119:165–168. The Bible affords us opportunities for praising God. Read Psalm 119:171–172.

- Recall the story of the wise man who built his house on a rock and the foolish man who built his house on the sand.

- Read Matthew 7:24: "Jesus said, 'Whoever hears these sayings of Mine, and does them, I will liken him to a wise man who built his house on the rock.'"

- Special music (solo or special group): "Wonderful Words of Life"

- God's Word does contain wonderful words of life. Don't just read it or quote it. Live it! Live it every day!

- Prayer

If you choose to do a craft, glue a Bible verse on a Bible shape.

Supplies:

- Open-Bible shapes drawn on black construction paper
- The words *wonderful words of life* typed on white copy paper
- Scissors
- Glue
- Clear plastic adhesive to cover the finished Bible

Cut out the Bible shapes, glue the typed words across the middle of the Bible shapes and cover with the clear plastic adhesive. Suggest that each person may wish to give his or her finished "Bible" to someone, reminding them that the Bible is God's Word – an important, special book.

The Story of Hosea

Suggested materials: Bibles, songbooks, the words and music to the song "The Love of God" and posterettes with the words beginning in B.

Devotional Time Suggestions

- Today, we will think together about God's great love for us.

- Songs: "Love Lifted Me" and "Jesus Loves Me"

- Prayer asking God's blessings on this devotional time.

- Song: "My Savior's Love"

- Special music (solo or special group): "The Love of God"

Hosea

The book of Hosea, one of the Minor Prophets in the Old Testament, contains the story of Hosea's love for Gomer.

Hosea was a man of God.

He fell deeply in love with Gomer, a young woman who, Bible scholars say, was part of an ungodly culture.

Several words beginning with the letter *B* describe the story of the marriage and life of Hosea and Gomer. (Ask several people to show the posterette when the correct *B* word is discussed)

Bright future:	They were two young adults beginning life and building a home together. Hosea loved Gomer. Life seemed good, and the future looked bright.
Blossoming love:	Hosea loved Gomer with all his heart, took care of her and gave her gifts.
Blessed marriage:	The family grew. Hosea and Gomer had three sons.

Blessings forgotten:	Gomer forgot the blessings she enjoyed as Hosea's wife. She went back to her old sinful ways, seeking the companionship of ungodly men who tempted her with empty promises. Gomer forgot the blessings she had at home. She turned her back on her faithful, hard-working and loving husband, Hosea.
Broken marriage:	Gomer left her marriage. She had a lover with whom she squandered the gifts that Hosea had given her.
Broken home:	Gomer not only left her marriage, she left her children.
Broken heart:	Hosea's heart was broken. He grieved about his love, his marriage, his home and his children. He made efforts to find Gomer and bring her home, but was unable to do so.
Bond slave:	When they were finished with her, Gomer's lovers left her with nothing – no home, no family, no self-respect, no money and no hope. Now she was chained to a slave block. She was to be sold as a slave to the highest bidder.

Gomer was dishonored and deserted. She had wasted her life and her youth. Her beauty had faded. She stood on the slave block dirty, disheveled, alone and worthless.

Bountiful love: At the sight of Gomer on the slave block, Hosea was completely devastated. The woman he deeply loved was pitiful and in such a deplorable condition. However, no matter what she had done or what condition she was in, Hosea's heart was beating with an undying love – an unending love.

Bought in love:	Hosea went to the slave market, where Gomer was put on the auction block. Hosea bought her. He paid for the now pitiful, dirty, sinful older woman who had been his beautiful young wife. He declared his love for her. He took her home. She would not be a slave, but his wife.
Beautiful, lasting love:	In the last chapter of the book of Hosea, God relates Hosea's broken marriage and disgraced home to a picture of God's heart as He calls His people to return to Him. God's love for you and me is unending. He made us. He loves us. When we were yet sinners, He "bought us back" by sending His Son to die for us. God loved us that much.

If you choose to do a craft, make February "heart people".

Supplies:

- Red, white and pink construction paper
- Several patterns for three sizes of hearts: one large (body), one medium (head), four smaller (arms and legs), one small for the heart
- Pencils
- Scissors
- Glue
- Thin-line marker
- Hole punch
- Ribbon or string

On a sheet of construction paper, ask each person to draw around the seven hearts needed to make a "heart person" (or cut them out ahead of time). Glue the medium heart (head) at the top of the large heart (body), glue the four smaller hearts (arms and legs) at the sides and bottom of the large heart, and glue the small heart on the left side of the body to give it a heart. Draw dot eyes and a smile on the head-heart. Punch a hole in the head, tie a string or ribbon through the hole and hang the heart people to sway in the air.

Valentines and Love

Suggested materials: Bibles, suggested scripture passages written on paper strips, old and/or new valentines (some romantic ones, some funny ones) on display; for the focal area, cut a large red heart from poster board

Devotional Time Suggestions

Ahead of time, give the scripture passage strips (and Bibles) to persons who are able and comfortable reading aloud.

- It is valentine time! Valentines are ways of expressing love and friendship. Show, talk about and read the displayed valentines.

- Someone tell us about giving valentines to classmates when you were in school. Did you make a valentine sack in which to put the valentines?

- Song: "Let Me Call You Sweetheart" This is a classic love song. There is another song called, "I'll Be Loving You Always." Do you remember it?

- Can any of you tell us about one of the best valentines you ever received? (Allow plenty of time for sharing stories)

Love

- I John 4:16 says "God is love." Love is God-given. Love for sweethearts is wonderful. But we all know about other kinds of love.

Love of God: The Pharisees asked Jesus "What is the great commandment?" He answered, "Thou shalt love The Lord thy God with all thy heart, and with all thy soul, and with all thy mind." (Matthew 22:37)

- First John 4:19 says "We love God because He first loved us."

- Love for God should be the primary and most important love in our lives.

Love of Family:	Love for your parents, love for your brothers and sisters, love for your spouse, love for your children, love for your grandchildren and great-grandchildren and love for your extended family – aunts, uncles and cousins.

First John 4:20 says, "If a man says, I love God, and hateth his brother, he is a liar: for he that loveth not his brother whom he seen, how can he love God whom he has not seen?"

Love of Others:	When Jesus answered about the great commandment of loving God, he added, "love thy neighbor as thyself." Loving others makes our lives better and more fulfilled. Life without friends would be a sad life, indeed. Someone has said, "To be loved by others, we must love others."

First John 4:7 – "...love one another for love is of God."

Valentines are wonderful because they help express our love to family and friends.

Our love is important and makes life sweeter for ourselves and for the ones we love. But the most wonderful love we have in our lives is the love we have for God. We love Him because He first loved us.

Our valentine to God can be a prayer of thanksgiving and love.

- Prayer: "Thank You, God, for loving us. We love you because you first loved us. Our hearts are filled with love for You when we remember that, while we were yet sinners, You sent Your Son to die for us. Thank You for Your love and that You have put in our hearts our love for You, for our families and for others.

If you choose to do a craft, make valentines.

Supplies:

- Red construction paper
- White copy paper
- Small white and silver doilies
- Glitter
- Envelopes
- Pencils and pens
- Scissors
- Glue
- Flower and heart stickers

Allow each person to make at least three valentines, to write a message of love in each one and to put each one in an envelope. You may want to provide one stamp for each person so that he or she can mail one of the handmade valentines. Encourage delivery of the valentines to close by friends.

Liberty! Presidents Day

Suggested materials: United States flag, Bible, words and music to the songs, "America" and "God Bless America", pencil and paper for one person to write down names of U.S. presidents, a set of United States coins, one-dollar bill, five-dollar bill, ten-dollar bill and a twenty- dollar bill

Devotional Time Suggestions

- Begin with special music (solo or special group): "America, America, God shed His grace on thee."

- Prayer thanking God for America.

- Song: "My Country, 'Tis of Thee"

- This month, a day is set aside to honor our past and present United States presidents called, "Presidents Day."

- As of 2011, 44 presidents have led our great country. Let's see how many of them you can name:

  George Washington
  John Adams
  Thomas Jefferson
  James Madison
  James Monroe
  John Quincy Adams
  Andrew Jackson
  Martin Van Buren
  William Henry Harrison
  John Tyler
  James Polk
  Zachary Taylor
  Millard Fillmore

Franklin Pierce
James Buchanan
Abraham Lincoln
Andrew Johnson
Ulysses Grant
Rutherford Hayes
James Garfield
Chester Arthur
Grover Cleveland
Benjamin Harrison
Grover Cleveland
William McKinley
Theodore Roosevelt
William Taft
Woodrow Wilson
Warren Harding
Calvin Coolidge
Herbert Hoover
Franklin Roosevelt
Harry Truman
Dwight Eisenhower
John F. Kennedy
Lyndon Johnson
Richard Nixon
Gerald Ford
Jimmy Carter
Ronald Reagan
George H.W. Bush
Bill Clinton
George W. Bush
Barack Obama

- Who is our current president? No matter what our political party affiliation is, we must pray for our president and the other leaders of our great country.

- Prayer asking for God's blessings and His guidance for America, for our president and for our other leaders.

- Songs: "America the Beautiful" and "Battle Hymn of the Republic"

- Just for fun, let's look at our United States coins. (hold them up as you mention them) Whose or what picture is on the penny? On the nickel? On the dime? On the quarter? On the fifty-cent piece? Now, let's look at our paper money. Whose or what picture is on the one-dollar bill? The five-dollar bill? The ten-dollar bill? The twenty-dollar bill?

- The Pharisees decided they would try to trick Jesus. They went to Him and asked, (Luke 20:20–22) "Is it lawful to pay tribute (taxes) to Caesar?" Caesar represented the government of that day. Jesus answered, (verse 24) "Show me a penny. Whose image and superscription is on it?" They answered that the image on the penny was that of Caesar. Then Jesus said, (verse 25) "Give therefore unto Caesar the things which be Caesar's and unto God that which is God's."

We have all fussed about taxes, but as Jesus told the people that day, we must pay our taxes to our government and we must also give to God. We can be thankful for our great country where we have freedom to live and worship God as we please.

- Prayer thanking God for our country and our freedom.

- Lead the group in saluting the American flag. Close with the song "God Bless America."

If you choose to do a craft, make a penny prayer reminder card.

Supplies:
- White no-line index cards
- Pennies
- Glue
- Red and blue thin-line felt markers

Ask each person to write the words *God Bless America* at the top of the card, and on the bottom of the card, write *Pray for Our Country*. Give instructions for each person to draw a border on their prayer reminder card with the red and blue markers.

You Gotta Have Heart

Suggested materials: Bible, songbooks and some "heart" decorations

Devotional Time Suggestions

Today, we are going to think about and talk about hearts. Give me some words, phrases and names of songs that have the word "heart" in them.

- God's heart is full of love for you and me. Let's sing the song, "Near to the Heart of God."

- Prayer

You Gotta Have Heart!

- You gotta have heart! Luke 10:27 says "Love the Lord thy God with all thy heart." We must open our hearts to what God wants to do through us. We need to say with the psalmist, "Create in me a clean heart, O God, and renew a right spirit within me." (Psalm 51:10) Matthew 5:8 says, "Blessed are the pure in heart."

- You gotta have heart! While God gives you life, make sure that your heart is *a loving heart*. First John 4:7 says, "Love one another, for love is of God." Someone has said, "Love makes the world go 'round." Victor Hugo wrote something like this: "The supreme happiness of life is to love and to know that you are loved."

- You gotta have heart! While God gives you life, make sure that your heart is *a happy heart*. Proverbs 17:22 says, "A merry heart does good like a medicine." Proverbs 15:13 says, "A merry heart makes a cheerful countenance." No one likes a person who constantly frowns, is cranky and obnoxious. You can be a happy, smiling individual that is loved and cherished.

- You gotta have heart! While God gives you life, make sure that your heart is *a confident heart*. A confident heart believes and trusts God when He says, "Let not your heart be troubled, neither let it be afraid." (John 14:27)

- You gotta have heart! While God gives you life, make sure that your heart is *a giving, encouraging heart.*

Hebrews 3:13 says, "...encourage one another day after day." Just a smile and a kind word of encouragement from you may change someone's life. Encouragement means to "give heart." A psychologist said that, like a plant needs water, people need encouragement.

- You gotta have heart! Half-heartedness isn't the key to a loving, happy, encouraging heart. The key to a loving heart, a happy heart, an encouraging heart is found in Luke 10:27: "Love the Lord thy God will all your heart."

- Avoid letting Satan steal your loving, happy, confident, encouraging heart. Keep on with daily, personal Bible study and prayer.

Along with the psalmist, say, "Let the words of my mouth and the meditation of my heart be acceptable in Thy sight, O Lord, my strength and my Redeemer." (Psalm 19:14)

- Song: "In My Heart There Rings a Melody"

- You gotta have heart!

- Prayer

If you choose to do a craft, make musical shakers.

Supplies:

- Various sizes of sterilized plastic bottles and containers (medicine bottles, soap bottles, juice and soda bottles, etc.)
- Dry rice
- Dried beans
- Popcorn
- Tape for securing the materials in the containers that don't have lids

Fill the containers with different amounts of the dry items and secure the lids. Shake the containers to keep time with music. Save the shakers to use again and again during group singing or while listening to music.

God's Peace

Suggested materials: Bible, songbook, the words and music to the song "Peace Be Still"

Devotional Time Suggestions

- Prayer

- Songs: "Brighten the Corner", "Blessed Assurance" and "No, Not One"

- Have you ever been in a bad storm? A tornado? A hurricane? A snowstorm? A sandstorm? Allow time for the participants to relate storm experiences.

- In the New Testament, Mark and Matthew both relate the story of Jesus teaching by the Sea of Galilee. The crowd grew so large that he stepped on a ship and continued to teach.

Read Mark 4:36–41, the story of Jesus quieting the storm. He only had to say, "peace, be still," and the storm ceased.

- All of us have or have had stormy times, difficult times, in our lives. The winds of change blow fiercely in our lives. The winds of bad times blast through our lives. The winds of life's upheavals put us in a deep fog. The winds of bad times, death, illness, disappointment, loneliness and unkindness come storming in when we least expect them. The storms of life *rage*!

- But we know who can still the storms in our lives. God can. He will bring the gentle breezes of joy and happiness in spite of the storms. God can and will give us peace and comfort. Psalm 29:11b says "...the Lord will bless his people with peace."

- When the storms come, we can pray and ask for God's help. A song has the message "When the storms of life are raging, Lord, stand by me!" Isaiah wrote, "God will keep him in perfect peace, whose mind is stayed on Him."

- There is an old story about an art contest. The winning artist would be the one who could paint the best picture that depicted "peace."

Artists painted all kinds of pictures depicting peaceful, green fields. Other artists painted pictures of beautiful, quiet gardens with flowers of all colors. Still others painted pictures of people sitting quietly, pondering magnificent, peaceful nature scenes of mountains.

But one painting won first place, the painting that the judges felt was the best depiction of "peace." It was a painting of a huge, roaring and raging waterfall. A tree limb hung above the tumultuous waterfall. On the limb sat a tiny little bird, whistling his song. In spite of the deafening storm of water cascading down, the little bird sat peacefully singing above the roaring falls.

- We can have that kind of peace. When the storms of life are raging, we know the one who can say, "Peace, be still!"

- In John 14:27, Jesus said, "Peace I leave with you, my peace I give unto you: not as the world giveth, give I unto you. Let not your heart be troubled, neither let it be afraid."

- God can and will give us peace. First Peter 5:7 says "Casting all your cares upon Him; for He cares for you."

- Prayer

- Song: "God Will Take Care of You"

If you choose to do a craft, make scripture balloons.

Supplies:
- Balloons (medium-sized)
- Small strips of paper on which is written *God cares for you (1 Peter 5:7)*
- Tank of helium gas (available for rent at party stores)

Stuff a scripture strip into each balloon, then blow up the balloon and tie it quickly so that the helium will not escape. When all of the balloons are filled, take them outdoors. Let them fly away in the wind. Pray that those who find the balloons will read the scripture messages and turn to God for help. If some participants are unable to go outdoors, hopefully they can sit by a window and watch their friends let the balloons fly away.

You Are Special

Suggested materials: Bible, songbooks and a large poster with the words God Made You Special

Devotional Time Suggestions

- Songs: "In the Garden" and "Open My Eyes"

- Prayer thanking God that He made each of us very special.

- On the front porch, a little girl was alone, playing with her dolls. A salesman stepped up on the porch and saw the child all by herself. He smiled and said "Hello, little girl. Aren't you lonesome playing there all by yourself?
"No," she replied, "I'm not lonesome. I like me!"

What a wonderfully healthy attitude the little girl had about herself!

- Often, we wonder why God has made us like we are. We look around and wish we were someone else.

- A woman said to her friend "I wish I were you." Her friend said "I would rather be what God chose to make me than the most glorious creature that I can think of. For God has thought about me! I was born in God's thoughts and then made by God. That is the grandest, most precious thing."

- Psalm 139:17: "How precious are Your thoughts to me, O God," the psalmist, David, was referring to God's thoughts about David at his conception; God's thoughts as He wove David together in his mother's womb.

- Read Psalm 139:1–10. God made each of us, knows each of us, is with us and will lead us.

- In Psalm 139:14, David declares to God "I will praise Thee; for I am fearfully and wonderfully made: marvelous are thy works, and that my soul knows right well."

- Please turn to the person next to you and say, "God made me. I am fearfully and wonderfully made!"

- You and I are not in this world by mistake. We are God's special creation. We can look at ourselves in the mirror and say with David, "I am fearfully and wonderfully made, Lord. Marvelous are your works."

- Psalm 139:17–18: "How precious it is, Lord, to realize that you are thinking about me constantly! I can't even count the times a day your thoughts turn toward me. And when I awaken in the morning, you are still thinking of me!"

- You are an original creation, made by God, the great designer. You are a one-of-a-kind design. You are dear, wonderful and precious to God. Anytime, anywhere, you can come to God.

- Song: "Just As I Am"

- Prayer of thanksgiving to God for making us and loving us.

If you choose to do a craft, make a "you are special" mirror.

Supplies:
- Colored poster board squares
- Small mirrors (may be purchased at hobby stores)
- Strips of white copy paper, on which is typed *You were designed by God. You are special.*
- Glue gun and glue (regular glue will not hold the mirrors as well and does not dry quickly)
- Scissors (if needed)
- Hole punch
- Ribbon

You may choose to have the squares precut or allow each person to cut out his or her own square. Glue the mirror on the square, then glue the word strip under the mirror. Punch a hole above the mirror and tie a ribbon through it to make a hanger.

Mother's Maxims and Bible Proverbs

Suggested materials: Bible with the suggested proverbs marked for easy access, each suggested Bible proverb printed in large black letters on a separate large poster board, a large easel, also on a large poster board the printed words Mother's Maxims and Bible Proverbs

Before the participants arrive, place the theme poster on the easel. As it is presented, place each proverb poster on the easel or wall.

Devotional Time Suggestions

- Prayer

- Songs: "O Happy Day" and "In My Heart There Rings a Melody"

Mother's Maxims

Think of some maxims or sayings that your parents or someone close to you often said. I will start by sharing a few maxims or sayings, and then it will be your time to share. Do you remember these? Read the first three:

> Idle hands are the devil's workshop.
> Don't bite off more than you can chew.
> It's as plain as the nose on your face.

If the group is slow to respond, share more maxims. After each one, give time for response that they did or didn't remember that one. Encourage fun and laughter.

> They're as scarce as hen's teeth.
> Don't cut off your nose to spite your face.
> Make hay while the sun shines.
> A whistling girl and a crowing hen always come to some bad end.
> Actions speak louder than words.
> Don't cross that bridge until you come to it.
> It's as easy as rolling off a log.

You can't see the forest for the trees.

Avoid making a mountain out of a molehill.

No use to lock the barn door after the horse is gone.

Two heads are better than one, even if one is a blockhead.

If you keep making that face, it will freeze that way.

Let sleeping dogs lie.

There's many a slip between the cup and the lip.

Strike while the iron is hot.

Keep a stiff upper lip.

Bible Proverbs

God gave us some Bible maxims. The book of Proverbs has all kinds of maxims, sayings and proverbs for us to live by. (As you read and talk about each proverb, place the printed proverb poster on the easel)

Proverbs 1:7a: "The fear of The Lord is the beginning of knowledge."

Proverbs 3:5: "Trust in the Lord with all your heart; and lean not unto your own understanding."

Proverbs 7:2: "Keep my commandments, and live: and my laws as the apple of thine eyes."

Proverbs 8:33: "Hear instruction, and be wise and refuse it not."

Proverbs 12:22: "Lying lips are an abomination to the Lord, but they that deal truly are His delight."

Proverbs 12:25: "Heaviness in the heart of man makes it stoop, but a good word makes it glad."

Proverbs 15:1: "A soft answer turns away wrath, but grievous words stir up anger."

Proverbs 15:13a: "A merry heart makes a cheerful countenance."

Proverbs 16:31: "A "gray" head is a crown of glory, if it be found in the way of righteousness."

Proverbs 17:22: "A merry heart does good like a medicine."

Proverbs 22:1a: "A good name is rather to be chosen than great riches."

Proverbs 25:11: "A word fitly spoken is like apples of gold in pictures of silver."

Proverb 26:20: "Where no wood is, there the fire goeth out, so when there is no talebearer, the strife ceases."

If you choose to do a craft, make pasta pictures.

Supplies:

- Paper plates or pieces of colored cardboard
- Large pasta in various shapes
- Glue
- Tempera paints
- Paint brushes.

On the paper plate, glue the pasta in a design. Paint the pasta to make a colored-design picture.

Characteristics of God

Suggested materials: Bible, songbooks, chalkboard, chalk, eraser or whiteboard and markers

Devotional Time Suggestions

- Song: "To God Be the Glory"

- Read Job 9:10: "God does great things, unfathomable, and wondrous works without numbers."

- Special Music: "How Great Thou Art"

- As we think about God and His greatness, let's think together about some of God's characteristics:

    Our God is *Powerful* – Psalm 62:11: "Power belongs to God."

    Our God is *Good* – Nahum 1:7: "The Lord is good, a strong hold in the day of trouble; and He knows them that trust in Him."

    Our God is *Loving* – John 3:16: "God so loved the world..."

- Song: "My Savior's Love"

    Our God is *Caring* – 1 Peter 5:7: "Casting all your cares upon Him; for He cares for you."

    Our God is *Comforting* – Psalm 34:18: "The Lord is nigh unto them that are of a broken heart; and saveth such as be of a contrite spirit."

    Our God is *Faithful* – Deuteronomy 7:9: "Know therefore that the Lord thy God, he is God, the faithful God."

- Song: "Great Is Thy Faithfulness"

    Our God is *Merciful* – Joel 2:13: "...the Lord your God: for He is gracious and merciful, slow to anger, and of great kindness."

- Song: "Amazing Grace"

Our God is *Unchanging* – Malachi 3:6: "I am The Lord, I change not."

Our God is *Eternal* – Deuteronomy 33:27: "The eternal God is they refuge, and underneath are the everlasting arms."

- Read Psalm 29:2: "Give unto The Lord the glory due unto His name."

- Song: "To God Be The Glory"

- Prayer of thankfulness to God for His love and goodness to us.

If you choose to do a craft, make stenciled postcards

Supplies:

- Thin postcard-size poster board
- Flower and/or animal stencils (available at craft stores)
- Dry tempera paint in several colors
- Sponges and brushes
- Masking tape

For each color, make a nearly dry paint. Mix only a small amount of water with tempera in a plate. Tape a stencil to a postcard. Carefully dip the sponge or brush in the paint. With the paint, fill in the inside of the stencil shape. Carefully remove the tape, lift off the stencil and see the design. If someone chooses to make more than one postcard, allow him or her to do so.

The Triumphal Entry of Jesus

Suggested materials: five Bibles – one for the leader and four for assigned readers.

On paper strips, write four reading assignments:

First reader – Mark 11:1–2

Second reader – Matthew 21:8–9

Third reader – Luke 19:38

Fourth reader – John 12:13

Give the assignments to four readers. (avoid embarrassing anyone who does not wish to read)

Devotional Time Suggestions

- Today, we are looking at a wonderful story – the story of Jesus' triumphal entry into the city of Jerusalem.

- Let's sing and praise Jesus, our Savior. Songs: "Jesus Saves" and "Jesus Is All the World to Me"

- Jesus spent many months going to the towns and villages of Palestine. Everywhere He went, He preached about the Kingdom of God. He healed the sick. It was springtime on the Sunday before His crucifixion. Jesus knew His earthly mission was almost finished. As He and His disciples traveled to Jerusalem, Jesus told His disciples that He would be killed and, after three days, He would rise again. Now it was time for Jesus to claim Himself to be the Messiah, the Savior that God had promised to the Jewish people.

- As Jesus and His disciples came to a small village near Jerusalem, He told two of His disciples to go into the village. (Ask the first reader to read Mark 11:1–2) The disciples found the colt (donkey), and the people let them have it because they were told that the Lord needed it.

- Jerusalem was crowded with pilgrims who had come for the annual Passover celebration. As Jesus rode into Jerusalem on the donkey, the crowds cheered. They spread their coats on the ground in front of Him. They waved branches of palm leaves.

  (Ask the second reader to read Matthew 21:8–9, the third reader to read Luke 19:38, the fourth reader to read John 12:13)

- As Jesus rode the donkey down the streets and passed the waiting crowds, the people shouted,

  "Hosanna!"

  "Blessed is the king who comes in the name of the Lord."

  "Blessed is the king of Israel."

- The people greeted Jesus as only a king would be greeted, but most of them misunderstood. They expected Jesus, their Messiah, to be a great political and military leader. They expected Jesus to lead them to victory over the oppression of the Romans. Jesus came, not to be king, but to redeem them – to redeem us. He came to save them – to save us, from our sins. He came to give them – to give us, eternal life.

- Four good lessons we can learn from this story of Jesus' triumphal entry into Jerusalem:

  1. As the owner of the donkey gave his animal because "the Lord needed it," so we can learn to obey God's instructions to us. We find God's instructions in God's Word, the Bible.

  2. We can learn to be willing for God to use us in any way He chooses, and be willing for God to use our possessions.

  3. We can learn that rejoicing and pain can be in our lives at the same time. Joyful, triumphant in His entry into Jerusalem, Jesus knew He was facing the cross. With God, our comforter and source of life, we can be triumphant in joy and in pain.

  4. But the best lesson of all is that Jesus is King, and we can give Him worship, honor, and praise.

- Through Jesus, we can have victory. Let's sing the song, "Victory in Jesus."

If you choose to do a craft, make crepe paper streamers.

Supplies:

- Twelve-inch long dowel sticks
- Five colors of crepe-paper strips
- Glue

Glue or tie several crepe paper strips to each dowel stick to make a "pom-pom" to wave and celebrate our "victory in Jesus."

Easter

Suggested materials: Bible, some springtime flowers (just for decoration), an Easter basket with eggs, a stuffed toy bunny rabbit and songbooks

Devotional Time Suggestions

- It is Easter! Happy Easter to all of you!

- When you were a child, how did your family celebrate Easter? Allow time for people to reply. If they hesitate, ask several to respond.

- Easter is much more than a symbol of springtime. Easter is more than baskets of eggs, bunnies, chocolate candy and Easter meals. Easter is a celebration of our Savior's crucifixion and resurrection from the grave. That should put a smile on our faces!

- Songs: "Redeemed" and "O Happy Day"

- All four of the Gospels – Matthew, Mark, Luke and John, record the death, burial and resurrection of Christ.

- At noon on the day that Jesus was crucified by Roman soldiers, an angry wind began to blow. Darkness covered the earth. An earthquake violently shook the earth. Jesus cried "It is finished." At that moment, the veil in the temple in Jerusalem was torn from top to bottom, opening the way to God through His Son's death for us.

Joseph of Arimathaea asked for the privilege and buried the body of Jesus in a new tomb. Three days after Jesus was buried, Jesus arose from the grave as He had said He would. Mary Magdalene and the other Mary (and maybe some other women) went to Jesus' tomb to put embalming spices on His body. They discovered that the stone had been rolled away from the tomb – and it was empty! An angel of the Lord said to them, "You seek Jesus of Nazareth, which was crucified: He is not here: behold the place where they laid Him." (Mark 16:6) The women rushed to tell Jesus' disciples that Jesus was alive!

- Jesus' resurrection was living proof that Jesus was *powerful*.

  In Matthew 28:18, Jesus said, "All power is given unto me in heaven and earth." Jesus can't fail! His resurrection is an indication of His power over sin, death, hell and evil. Satan cannot defeat Jesus' purpose, His saving power. All-powerful Jesus was crucified and arose from the grave to save us from our sins.

- Jesus' resurrection was *personal*.

  Second Corinthians 5:14–15: "For the love of Christ constraineth us; because we thus judge, that if one died for all, then were all dead: And that He died for all, that they which live should not henceforth live unto themselves, but unto him which died for them, and rose again."

- Jesus' resurrection was *permanent*.

  Jesus' crucifixion and resurrection are as valid today as they were more than 2,000 years ago. Jesus, our Savior, died on the cross for our sins and is now our living God.

- Songs: "He Is Lord" and "He Lives"

- Prayer thanking God for sending His Son whose death and resurrection were powerful, personal for us, and permanent.

If you choose to provide a craft, decorate Easter eggs

Supplies:

- Eggs (either hard-boiled eggs or colored plastic eggs)
- Either egg cold-water dye and the necessary accessories for coloring real eggs or bits of ribbon
- Lace
- Rick rack
- Beads
- Glue
- Other items for decorating plastic eggs

If you choose to decorate real hard-boiled eggs, you may want to ask the kitchen staff to supply the eggs and serve them for lunch or dinner. If you choose to decorate colored plastic eggs, allow each person to select the provided decorations that he chooses to glue on his or her egg.

Because He Lives

Suggested materials: Bible, songbooks and a poster with the words Because He Lives

Devotional Time Suggestions

- Because Jesus was crucified and arose from the grave, and because He lives, we have much about which to sing.

- Songs: "I Love to Tell the Story" and "He Lives"

- Special Music (solo or a group of singers): "Because He Lives"

Because He Lives

- *Because Jesus lives, I can face tomorrow.*

  Quote John 3:16: "For God so loved the world that he gave his only begotten Son, that whosoever believeth in Him should not perish but have everlasting life." Then ask the group to quote it with you.

  - Because He lives, we can handle and face the rest of our lives.

    - In John 14:1, Jesus said, "Let not your heart be troubled, you believe in God, believe also in Me."

    - Philippians 4:13: "I can do all things through Christ who strengthens me."

  - Because He lives, we can live and remember good times and joy.

    - John 16:24 says, "...ask and you shall receive, that your joy may be full."

    - Psalm 4:7: "God has put gladness in my heart."

    - Psalm 16:11: "God will show me the path of life: in Your presence is fullness of joy; at Your right hand there are pleasures evermore."

- Because He lives, we can lean on Him and face bad times and sorrow. Psalm 37:23–24: "The steps of a good man are ordered by the Lord: and he delights in His way. Though He fall, he shall not be utterly cast down: for the Lord upholds him in His hand."

- *Because Jesus lives, all fear is gone.*

  - Because He lives, we don't have to be afraid.

    - John 14:27b: "Let not your heart be troubled, neither let it be afraid."

    - In John 14:1–3, Jesus said: "Let not your heart be troubled: you believe in God, believe also in Me. In My Father's house are many mansions: if it were not so I would have told you. I go to prepare a place for you. And if I go and prepare a place for you, I will come again, and receive you unto Myself; that where I am, there you may be also."

    - Proverbs 3:5: "Trust in The Lord with all your heart; and lean not unto your own understanding."

    - Psalm 37:1–2: "Fret not thyself because of evildoers, neither be thou envious against the workers of iniquity. For they shall soon be cut down like grass, and wither as the green herb. Trust in The Lord, and do good; so shalt you dwell in the land, and you shall be fed."

    - Proverbs 29:25: "The fear of man brings a snare: but whoso puts his trust in The Lord shall be safe."

- *Because Jesus lives, I know He holds the future.*

  - Because He lives, we can trust Him with our future.

    - Proverbs 16:20b: "…whoso trusts in The Lord, happy is he."

    - Isaiah 26:4: "Trust in the Lord forever: for in The Lord Jehovah is everlasting strength."

    - Proverbs 9:11: "For by me (God) your days shall be multiplied, the years of your life shall be increased."

    - Isaiah 46:4: "Even to your old age I am (God); and even to (grey) hairs will I carry you: I have made, and I will bear; even will I carry, and deliver you."

- Proverbs 3:6: "I all your ways acknowledge Him (God), and He shall direct your paths."

- How wonderful that because he lives, we can face tomorrow, all fears are gone and we know who holds the future.

- Special music (solo or group again sings): "Because He Lives"

If you choose to provide a craft, make a yellow happy face.

Supplies:
- Yellow paper or poster board
- Twelve-inch long circles to use as patterns
- Colored permanent markets
- Hole punches
- Yellow ribbon

Ask participants to use the circle patterns to cut circles out of the yellow paper. With the markers, draw happy faces on the yellow circles. Around the bottom of the happy faces, write *Because Jesus Loves.*

Psalm 1/Trees

Suggested materials: Bible and songbooks

Devotional Time Suggestions

Songs: "In The Garden" and "God Leads Us Along"

- God has made us a wonderful world! On the third day of creation, He created trees. Help me name some kinds of trees.

  We are blessed to have God's wonderful creation of trees.

- Now, help me with some songs, phrases or words with the word "tree" (work to involve the seniors and make it fun)

Suggestions:

- "Don't Sit Under the Apple Tree with Anyone Else but Me"
- Family tree
- "Oh, Christmas Tree"
- The acorn doesn't fall far from the tree
- "Rock-a-bye Baby on the Tree Top"
- Christmas tree
- "Tie a Yellow Ribbon Round The Old Oak Tree"
- Tree of life (garden of Eden)
- "Little Playmate, Come Out and Play with Me, Climb up My Apple Tree"
- Great oaks from little acorns grow

Trees

- Read Psalm 1:1–3. In this psalm, the psalmist compares a godly person to a "tree planted by rivers of water."

Trees need water in order to grow. Christians need the "living water" of Christ's salvation.

- John 4 contains the story of the Samaritan woman who met Jesus at Jacob's well in Samaria.

- Jesus asked the woman for a drink. The woman asked how Jesus could ask her for drink, since Jews and Samaritans didn't get along. Jesus answered, "If you knew the gift of God, and who it is that said to you 'Give me to drink'; you would have asked of Him, and He would have given you living water." Jesus also said, "Whosoever drinks of this water shall never thirst again." Jesus clarified his offer. Physical water can only satisfy physical thirst and you have to keep drinking. Jesus offered a source of spiritual life, living water, which will not only satisfy spiritual thirst forever, but will supply plenty for sharing with others.

The tree by "rivers of water" has a constant source of strength for growth. When we drink of living water, God's salvation, we have spiritual strength now and for eternity.

Trees bear fruit. Christians can "be fruitful in every good work."

- Matthew 12:33b: "...a tree is known by its fruit."

- Apple trees grow apples. Peach trees grow peaches. Oak trees grow acorns.

- We Christians grow in our spiritual lives. Colossians 1:10: "That you might walk worthy of the Lord unto all pleasing, being fruitful in every good work, and increasing in the knowledge of God."

Trees need deep roots and nutrients to be strong and bear fruit. Christians need spiritual nutrients. Our roots must be deep in personal relationship with God:

- In personal reading and knowing God's Word, the Bible

- In personal prayer

- In living a godly life

Trees grow from tiny seeds. Christians sow Gospel seeds.

- Our duty as Christians is to share the seeds of the Gospel.

- We do only the sowing, sharing the seeds of the God's plan.

- Read Jesus' parable of the seed. (Matthew 13:3–9, 18–23)

- Reread Psalm 1:1–3 and then close with the song "Just a Closer Walk with Thee."

- Prayer

If you choose to provide a craft, make a lead collage.

Supplies:

- Lots of different types of leaves (ahead of time, some of the seniors may enjoy gathering leaves)
- Large poster board
- Glue

Give each person a small pile of leaves. Make a collage by gluing the leaves on the poster board. Initiate conversation about trees and the thoughts in the devotional time.

A Springtime Garden

Suggested materials: Bible, songbooks and a bouquet of various live springtime flowers

Devotional Time Suggestions

- This is a wonderful time of year. Springtime, gardens and flowers go together.

- Songs: "Tis So Sweet to Trust in Jesus" and "Glory to His Name"

- God did make us a beautiful world!

- Did you learn the nursery rhyme "Mary, Mary quite contrary, how does your garden grow?" Let the seniors finish the rhyme: "With slider bells and cockle shells and pretty maids all in a row."

Why we plant

- Why do people plant gardens? (Allow time for answers)

- For enjoyment of color and beauty, we plant flowers of all kinds. (Name some colorful flowers that you have planted and enjoyed)

- For food, we plant vegetables and fruit bushes and trees.

- For privacy, we plant hedges.

- For shade, we plan large plants and trees.

- Why do we plant the garden of our lives?

- Just for our own selfish enjoyment, not caring for anyone else

- Just for today, with no thought of tomorrow

- Or to please God and glorify Him in your life and for eternity

- To make life better and happier for your family and friends

- To give encouragement and lift the spirits of others

What we plant

- What you plant in your garden makes a difference in the kind of garden you have.

- If you choose to grow roses, you have to plant rose bushes.

- If you choose to grow vegetables, you have to plant vegetable seeds.

- What we plant in the garden of our lives because the harvest depends on what we plant!

- In your life, you grow what you plant.

- Galatians 6:7: "Whatsoever a person sows, he shall also reap."

- When you plant complete trust in Jesus as your personal Savior, you reap eternal life.

- What we do and what we plant in our lives every day determines what we will reap each day.

One fellow said "My wife probably won't be happy in heaven. She has already done all her harping down here."

When we plant

- When we plant flowers and vegetables, it has to be in the correct season of the year.

- We don't plant flowers in freezing cold weather.

- The temperature has to be right for planting any flowers and vegetables.

- The planting time is short.

- When you plant in your life's garden, it needs to be *now*.

- Ecclesiastes 3:2: "There is…a time to plant."

- The time to plant in your life's garden is now, even when you are busy, even when you don't feel well.

- The planting time in your life's garden is short.

- Your season for growth and blooming is now, while you are living.

- Now is the time for you to think of what you can do for the Lord. You can pray. You can give time and effort, hugs. You can plant encouragement, a smile, a happy outlook, a sweet spirit.

How we plant

- Poor planting makes a sorry flower and vegetable garden.

- It takes the right soil. It takes cultivation, watering and weeding. It takes work on your knees and dedication to keep at it.

- Poor planting in our life gardens makes for unhappiness for you and for others around you.

- Don't let the weeds of neglect choke out your Christian life's garden.

- Satan stands by to choke out your joy and make you critical, grumpy and mean-spirited. Don't let him in your garden!

- With personal prayer, Bible study and trust in God, keep your life's garden well-kept and wonderful.

If you choose to provide a craft, make large crepe paper flowers.

Supplies:

- Several colors of crepe paper
- Green chenille sticks
- Green yarn
- Scissors

Cut large crepe paper petal shapes, twist the small end of the petal and tie it to a chenille stick stem. Keep tying petals to the stem to form a flower.

MAY – SECOND WEEK

Mothers

Suggested materials: Bible and songbooks

Devotional Time Suggestions

- This is the time of year when we honor and give special recognition to our mothers. Ask "how many of you are mothers?" Laugh and ask, "how many of you had a mother?" Of course! God gave us our mothers.
- Let's sing some songs that our mothers probably loved: "Amazing Grace" and "What a Friend We Have in Jesus"
- Our mother is special to every one of us. What are some words that come to mind when you think of a wonderful Christian mother? (Give time for answers)
- Prayer thanking God for our mothers
- Special Music (solos or group of musicians): A song that mothers have loved – "Savior, like a Shepherd Lead Us"
- A quiz about mothers in the Bible. As each question is answered about a mother, discuss her story:

  Who was the mother of Jacob and Esau? Rebekah

  Who was the mother of Moses, Aaron and Miriam? Jochebed

  Who was the mother of Joseph and Benjamin? Rachel

  Who was the mother of Samuel? Hannah

  Who was the mother of John the Baptist? Elizabeth

  Who was the mother of Jesus? Mary

  Who was the mother of Timothy? Lois

  Timothy's grandmother? Eunice

- Read and discuss these scriptures about mothers and godly women:
  - Titus 2:4–5
  - 2 Timothy 1:5
  - Proverbs 31:10–12 and 25–31
  - Proverbs 14:1
  - Psalm 127:3
- Song: "Leaning on the Everlasting Arms"
- Prayer

If you choose to provide a craft, make picture place mats

Supplies:
- Magazine pictures or personal photographs
- Poster board or construction paper
- Glue
- Clear contact paper

Glue the chosen picture(s) on the poster board or construction paper. Make a place mat by covering both sides of the board or paper with clear contact paper. Some may choose to make more than one place mat.

Elkanah, Hannah, Samuel

Suggested materials: Bible and songbooks

Devotional Time Suggestions

- Songs: "He Keeps Me Singing" and "God Will Take Care of You"

- Today, we are going to recall the story of the family of Elkanah. His wife, Hannah, prayed the following prayer in 1 Samuel 2:2: "There is none holy as The Lord: for there is none beside Him: neither is there any rock like our God."

- Special Music (solo or group of musicians): "I Need Thee Every Hour"

- The story of Elkanah and Hannah is a testimony of a need for God, praying to God, God's faithfulness and keeping promises to God.

The story is in 1 Samuel 1:

Hannah was the wife of a man, Elkanah. Elkanah and Hannah loved and served God. Hannah wanted children, but seemingly could not conceive a child. Every year, Elkanah and Hannah went to Shiloh to worship God and make sacrifices to Him.

Hannah was unhappy, desperately wanting a child. While she and her husband were at the house of God in Shiloh, Hannah cried, prayed and would not eat.

Elkanah asked why she was crying and why she wouldn't eat. He asked "Why is your heart grieved? Am I not better to you than ten sons?" Bitterly, Hannah continued to pray and weep.

As she prayed, she vowed to God and said "O Lord of hosts, if you will look on the affliction of your handmaid, and remember me, and not forget your handmaid, but will give your handmaid a man child, then will I give him unto the Lord all the days of his life, and shall no razor come upon his head."

God answered Hannah's prayer. She had a son and named him Samuel. God answered her prayer and she kept her promise to God. When her baby boy was weaned (some scholars say he was probably four or five years old, others say he was older), she and Elkanah returned to worship again at Shiloh. As Hannah had promised God, she "gave him unto the Lord." In order that Samuel could serve the Lord "all the days of his life," Hannah and Elkanah left Samuel to be a helper to the priest Eli at the house of worship.

- Hannah prayed and promised God that, if she had a child, she would bring her child to serve Him. She kept her promise. God answered her prayer.

- What does this story relate to you and me? It demonstrates that we have a loving God who listens to us and cares for us. Hannah's story demonstrates to us that we should keep our promises to God. We have a loving God who listens to us and cares for us. It demonstrates to us that God is faithful to keep His promises. We can count on Him. We can lean on Him.

- Song: "Standing On The Promises of God"

- Prayer

If you choose to do a craft, make a feeder for springtime birds.

Supplies:
- Pinecones
- Lard or shortening
- Table knives
- Glue gun
- Glue
- String

Using a table knife, "ice" the pinecones with the lard or shortening. Be sure that the pinecone layers are full. Cut a length of string, double it, and glue the two string ends to the top of the pinecones. Hang the "feeder" in an area where the birds can be watched.

Godly Attitudes

Suggested materials: Bible and songbooks

Devotional Time Suggestions

- Songs: Jesus Is All the World to Me" and "He Keeps Me Singing"

Attitudes

- The dictionary gives the definition of "attitudes" as a manner of acting, feeling or thinking that shows ones disposition, our feelings, our sentiments.

  What are some negative attitudes?

  - Frustration, anger, selfishness, the blahs, the blues, violence, hate, disrespect and unkindness

  Have you ever met anyone whose attitude is so negative that folks don't like to be around them?

  What are some positive attitudes?

  - Joy, delight, acceptance, love, kindness, giving, unselfishness, helpfulness, thoughtfulness, positive self-worth, thankfulness and forgiveness

  It is good to meet someone whose attitudes are positive, loving, kind and happy.

- One fellow said, "Folks are about as happy as they make up their minds to be."

- A story:

  The only survivor of a shipwreck was washed up on a small, uninhabited island. He prayed feverishly for God to rescue him. Every day he scanned the horizon for help, but none seemed forthcoming. Exhausted, he eventually managed to build a little hut out of driftwood. He and his meager belongings were protected from sun and rain. One day while scavenging for food, he discovered that his hut was on fire. He was stunned with grief and anger...everything was lost! He cried, "God, how could you do this to me?" The next day, he was awakened by the sound of a ship that was approaching the island. It had come to rescue him. The weary fellow asked, "How did you know I was here?" "We saw your smoke signal," was the reply.

- Discouragement comes easily when things are going badly, but we shouldn't lose heart, because God is at work in our lives, even in the midst of pain and heartache.

  - For all the negative things we have to say, God has a positive answer:

  - We say, "It's impossible." God says, "All things are possible." (Luke 18:27)

  - We say, "I'm too tired." God says, "I will give you rest." (Matthew 11:28–30)

  - We say, "Nobody really loves me." God says, "I love you." (John 3:16, 13:34)

  - We say, "I can't go on." God says, "My grace is sufficient." (2 Corinthians 12:9, Psalm 91:15)

  - We say, "I can't do it!" God says, "You can do all things." (Philippians 4:13)

  - We say, "I am afraid." God says, "I have not given you a spirit of fear." (2 Timothy 1:7)

- One of the only things that is truly yours is your attitude. No one else can control your attitude or take it from you.

- Remember, attitudes are contagious! Your attitude, good or bad, rubs off on the people around you. Every day, you have the choice to trust God. You have the choice to either have a good day or a bad day.

- Song: "He Keeps Me Singing"

- Prayer: "Lord, keep us kind, keep us loving. Help us make this a happy day, no matter what the circumstances."

If you choose to provide a craft, make an encouragement chain.

Supplies:
- Bright red and bright yellow construction paper
- Scissors
- Thin-line black felt markers
- Glue

- A poster with six Bible references which are positive answers from God: Luke 18:27, Matthew 11:28–30, John 3:16, Psalm 91:15, Philippians 4:13 and 2 Timothy 1:7

Cut out construction paper strips to make chain links. Write a Bible reference on each chain link. Glue the ends of the first strip together to make a circle link, put the end of the next link through the first one and glue the two ends, etc. to make a long chain. The same six Bible references can be used over and over on the paper chain links. Hang the chain on a wall. Place the poster over the chain.

Naomi, Ruth and Boaz

Suggested materials: Bible and songbooks

Devotional Time Suggestions

- Song: "Just a Closer Walk with Thee"

- Prayer

The Bible Story in the Book of Ruth

Naomi's Family Moved to Moab from Bethlehem.

A famine in Bethlehem forced Naomi, her husband and her two sons to move to Moab. Naomi's husband died. Her two sons married, but, soon both of her sons also died. Her daughters-in-law, Orpah and Ruth, loved Naomi.

Naomi Decided to Return to Bethlehem.

Naomi heard that, back in her hometown of Bethlehem, the famine was over. She decided to go back to Bethlehem. She insisted that the two daughters-in-law stay in Moab. Orpah stayed, but Ruth insisted on going with Naomi.

Ruth said, "Entreat me not to leave thee, or to return from following after thee: for whither thou goest, I will go: and where thou lodgest, I will lodge: thy people shall be my people, and thy God my God. Where thou diest, I will die, and there will I be buried; The Lord do so to me, and more also, if anything but death part thee and me." (Ruth 1:16-17)

Naomi and Ruth Went to Bethlehem.

In barley harvest time, they reached Bethlehem. Naomi was happily greeted. They were destitute and had no food. Naomi saw that the beautiful Ruth met Boaz, a "mighty man of wealth" who was a kinsman of Naomi's husband.

Ruth Gleaned Barley in Boaz's Field.

The custom was for the reapers to leave some grain in the fields for the poor people to glean so that they could have food. Boaz was a close relative of Naomi's husband. When Boaz saw Ruth, he insisted that she glean barley only in his fields and that, at mealtime, she'd come and eat with him. He gave orders for the gleaners to leave extra grain for Ruth to glean. Ruth took home enough grain for her and Naomi to have plenty of food. Ruth kept gleaning in Boaz's fields. He discovered that he loved Ruth.

Boaz's and Ruth's Love Blossomed into Marriage.

Boaz was not Naomi's closest relative, the one that had the right to marry Ruth. In front of the men of the town, Boaz went to Naomi's closest relative and asked permission to marry Ruth. The relative consented and told Boaz that he could buy the inheritance of Naomi's husband and the privilege of marrying Ruth.

With the blessing of Naomi, Ruth and Boaz marry. "So Boaz took Ruth and she was his wife." (Ruth 4:13) The Lord gave them a son whom they named Obed.

Naomi became nurse to Obed.

Naomi's friends said, "Blessed by the Lord, which hath not left thee this day without a kinsman, that his name shall be famous in Israel. He shall be unto thee a restorer of thy life, and a nourisher of thy old age: for thy daughter-in-law which loveth thee, which is better to thee than seven sons, hath borne him. And Naomi took the child, and laid it in her bosom, and became nurse to him." (Ruth 4:14-16)

Ruth's son, Obed, grew up and had a son.

Obed's son was named Jesse, who was the father of David. Jesus was in the lineage of David, as was Ruth, David's great-grandmother.

- The love of Ruth for Naomi and Boaz's love for Ruth are wonderful stories of love. It is a wonderful story of God's love and provision. God honored Naomi's wisdom and stamina in difficult times.

Special Music: "Blessed Assurance"

- Prayer

If you choose to provide a craft, make thumbprint flowers.

Supplies:

- White copy paper
- Colored stamp pads
- Several colors of thin-line felt markers

Demonstrate by pressing your thumb on one of the stamp pads and pressing your thumb on paper to make a flower petal. Make several thumbprint petals to form a flower. Use a marker to make the middle of the flower, flower stem and leaves. Help each person make a thumbprint flower (or a bouquet of flowers) on his or her paper. Encourage mixing and matching colors.

Blessings from God

Suggested materials: Bible, songbooks, a large poster board (or white board), at the top of which is printed Blessings from God, an easel and wide black marker

Devotional Time Suggestions

- During this time, let's think about God's blessings to us.

- Song: "Count Your Blessings"

- Prayer thanking God for all of His blessings to us.

- Often, we get so caught up in everyday living that we forget to count our blessings. Tell me some of the blessings that God has given us and you. I (or appoint someone) will write your answers on the board.

  (Allow lots of time for answers. To stimulate brainstorming, interject some blessings that might not be mentioned: a bed to sleep in, running water, shoes, doctors and nurses, hands, eyes, the Bible, the United States, freedom, happy memories, salvation, etc. Hopefully you can fill the board with listing blessings the seniors mention.)

- Sing the chorus: "Count your blessings, name them one by one. Count your many blessings, see what God has done."

- Luke 17:11-19 is the story of Jesus healing ten lepers:

  As Jesus was going to Jerusalem, he passed through a village where he was met by ten lepers, who stood far away from Him. Leprosy was and is a dreaded disease. Because leprosy was so contagious, lepers were not allowed to come in contact with other people.

  The ten lepers called to Jesus and said, "Jesus, Master, have mercy on us." When Jesus saw the lepers, he said to them "Go and show yourselves to the priests." Then in verse 15, it says "...as they went, they were cleansed." They were healed. One of the lepers, when he realized that Jesus had healed him, turned back and loudly glorified God. Verse 16 says "he fell down on his face at Jesus' feet, giving him thanks."

Jesus said, "Were there not ten cleansed? Where are the other nine?" He asked, "Was no one, except this man, this Samaritan, found that returned to give praise, and glory, and thanksgiving to God?" The ungratefulness of the nine, who were healed but didn't return to even say 'thanks,' must have filled Jesus' heart with sadness at their thoughtlessness.

They were healed from the dreaded leprosy, but didn't bother to even be grateful.

- Before we get too judgmental about their ungratefulness, we need to look at ourselves. We have named so many wonderful blessings that God has given us. Yet we often are not thankful enough to stop and thank God for His blessings. He has given us life and care and so many blessings we just take for granted.

- Jesus didn't owe the lepers anything, but he healed them. God doesn't owe us anything, but he loves us enough to pour out his blessings on us.

- Again, sing the chorus: "Count your blessings, name them one by one, count your many blessings, see what God has done."

- Prayer of thanksgiving (naming many of the blessings written on the poster board).

- Close with singing, "There Shall Be Showers of Blessings"

If you choose to provide a craft:

Supplies:

- Large white poster board
- Red marker
- Washable black marker
- Tape or sticky tack
- Either large flower stickers or pictures of flowers
- Glue

Place the poster board on a table. With the red marker, draw a border around the outside edge of the board, and write *I am thankful for:* at the top. Ask each person to write or draw on the board three to five things for which he or she is thankful to God. Allow each person to glue a flower picture or a sticker in and around the writing on the poster board. In a prominent place, display the finished poster on the wall.

Fathers

Suggested materials: Bible and songbooks

Devotional Time Suggestions

- Prayer and song: "A Child of the King"

Fathers

- This is the time of year when we honor and give special recognition to our fathers. Ask "how many of you are fathers?" Laugh and ask, "how many of you had a father?" Of course! God gave us our fathers.

- Name some characteristics of a Christian father. Allow time for answers. Tell us about a good memory of your father.

Luke 15:11–32 contains a story of a father's love:

A rich man had two sons. The younger son came to his father and demanded his share of the inheritance. His father split the assets and gave his youngest son his share of the assets.

The younger son left home. Probably gleefully, the younger son packed his bags and traveled to a distant land. He was on top of the world. He had money, and he spent it lavishly on wild parties and on people he thought were his friends. In a very short time, he had spent every penny of his inheritance. His new friends abandoned him. He was alone. He had no money. He was in a foreign land where he was a stranger with no one to turn to for help.

Meanwhile, a famine spread through the land. There were no jobs to be had and no food to be found. Finally desperate, the young man took a job feeding pigs, the most humiliating job he could possibly get. He was so hungry he wanted to eat what the pigs were eating. No one was willing to help him.

The boy thought, 'My father's hired servants had more than enough to eat, and here I sit alone and dying of hunger. I am going home! I will say to my father, "I have sinned against heaven and before you; I am no longer worthy to be called your son; treat me like one of your hired servants." (Luke 15:18-19)

The younger son, ashamed and defeated, went home to his father. But while he was still a distance away, his father saw him and, filled with love, ran to his son, embraced him and kissed him. The son said to his father, "Father, I have sinned against heaven and before you; I am no longer worthy to be called your son."

But the father would have none of that. He called his servants and asked them to quickly bring the best robe and put it on him. He put a ring on his son's finger and shoes on his feet. The father said to the servants, "Bring the fatted calf and kill it. And let us eat and make merry." In other words, let's have a party!

The older son, who had stayed at home and worked and never disobeyed his father, was angry and wouldn't go in to the party for his brother. He said that his father had never given him a party. He said, "But when his son or yours came, who has devoured your living with harlots, you killed for him the fatted calf!" (Luke 15:30)

His father answered, "Son, you are always with me, and all that is mine is yours. It was fitting to make merry and be glad, for this your brother was dead, and is alive; he was lost and is found." (Luke 15:31–32)

This story of the loving father is a parable that Jesus told. A parable is an earthly story with a heavenly meaning. It illustrates God's love for us, even when we are sinners. God has an incredible capacity to love and forgive. It shows God's compassion for those who repent, who admit their sins and ask for forgiveness. The older son represents anyone who lets pride or resentment stand in their way of their rejoicing with God at the return of someone who is lost.

Like with the older brother, all we have to do is ask our Father God for anything we need. We must not miss anything that God has provided for us.

- Special music (solos or group): "Love Divine"

- Close with reading Psalm 103:13: "God is like a father to us, tender and sympathetic to those who reverence Him."

If you choose to provide a craft, make wet chalk drawings.

Supplies:
- Chalk soaked for ten minutes in six tablespoons sugar and mixed in one-quarter cup of water
- White paper and colored paper.

Draw on the white paper with colored chalk. Draw on the colored paper with white chalk.

A Sing-Along Songfest

Suggested materials: Bibles and songbooks

Devotional Time Suggestions

- Begin with singing "I Will Sing of My Redeemer"

- Explain that today will a sing-along songfest and the seniors will choose the songs.

- Read (or assigned to be read) these scriptures:

  - "The Lord is my strength and my song" (Psalm 118:14)

  - "...with my song I will praise God" (Psalm 28:7)

  - "God has put a new song in my mouth" (Psalm 40:3a)

- Using the songbook, ask seniors to choose three songs for the group to sing. Sing only the first stanzas of the songs.

- Read (or assign to be read) these scriptures:

  - "I will praise the name of God with a song, and will magnify Him with thanksgiving." (Psalm 69:30)

  - "I will sing a new song unto Thee, O God" (Psalm 144:9)

- Ask seniors to choose three more songs to sing. Sing only the first stanzas of the songs.

- Read (or assign to be read) these scriptures:

  - "They sung a new song, saying, Thou art worthy to take the book, and to open the seals thereof, for thou wast slain, and hast redeemed us to God by the blood out of every kindred, and tongue, and people, and nation." (Revelation 5:9)

  - "Let the word of Christ dwell in you richly in all wisdom; teaching and admonishing one another in Psalms and hymns and spiritual songs, singing with grace in your hearts to the Lord." (Colossians 3:16)

- Sing two more songs (from the songbook) that the group chooses.

- Mention that the dictionary definition of a "psalm" is a song sung with harp accompaniment. When we read the Psalm 23, we can imagine David's playing on his harp and singing about the Lord. Ask the group to quote Psalm 23 together.

- Song: "God Leads Us Along"

- Prayer thanking God for the joy of singing His praises.

If you choose to provide a craft, make large music notes with the words *God Gives Me a Song*.

Supplies:
- A sheet of black construction paper for each person
- Large music note patterns as tall and wide as a construction paper sheet
- Word strips - white paper strips on which are written the words *God Gives Me a Song*
- Glue
- Scissors
- Pencils

Give each person a sheet of construction paper and a word strip. Place several large music note patterns on the work area. Tell the seniors to, on the black paper, draw around a music note pattern and cut out the note shape. On the cut-out note shape, glue a word strip.

Let Freedom Ring

Suggested materials: Bible, songbooks, patriotic decorations (red, white and blue), a large flag, small flags or patriotic crepe paper streamers for each participant, the music and words to the song, "God Bless America"

If you choose to do some refreshments to celebrate, be aware of salt free/sugar free diets.

Devotional Time Suggestions

- God is good to allow us to live in America where we can live without fear, can freely worship God and have freedom.

- Prayer of thankfulness for our country and for our freedom.

- Special Music (solo or a group): "God Bless America"

  Ask the participants to wave their flags or streamers during this song.

  Ask the musician(s) to sing the song again and invite the seniors to sing along.

- Ask these questions for the seniors to answer:

- From what country did the United States win independence? England

- Who rode through the countryside to warn the people that "the British are coming?" Paul Revere

- What day do we celebrate our freedom? July 4th

- What else is July 4th called? Independence Day

- Who was our first president and is called "The Father of Our Country?" George Washington

- Which president is known for being raised in a log cabin and for freeing the slaves? Abraham Lincoln

- Who made the first stars and stripes American flag? Betsy Ross

- Who wrote the national anthem, "The Star Spangled Banner?" Francis Scott Key

- Who said, "Give me liberty or give me death"? Patrick Henry

- In what city are Independence Hall and the Liberty Bell located? Philadelphia

- Who said, "Ask not what your country can do for you, ask what you can do for your country?" John F. Kennedy

- Who is our current United States President? (name the current president)

- Song: "My Country 'Tis of Thee"

Ask the seniors to wave their flags or streamers as they sing.

- Ask the participants to tell the freedoms for which they are most thankful.

- We celebrate our freedom on Independence Day. Remember those who have given their lives to assure and protect our freedom. How many of you have family members who have sacrificed themselves protecting our country? Let's pray a prayer of thankfulness to God for these brave soldiers, sailors, marines and others who have made the ultimate sacrifice for our freedom.

- Prayer thanking God for those men and women who have given their lives to protect our freedom.

- Today around the world, there are military men and women fighting and protecting our country and our freedoms.

- Prayer thanking God for our military personnel and praying for their safety.

- Salute the flag of the United States.

- Closing song: "Battle Hymn of the Republic"

If you choose to provide a craft, make patriotic flower pots.

Supplies:
- Small terra cotta flower pots
- Red, white and blue tempera paint
- Paint brushes
- Bowls of water brush cleaning
- Clear plastic spray

Give each person a terra cotta flower pot. Allow them to paint their own red, white and blue designs on the pots. Spray the pots with clear spray when they are finished painting.

Hands

Suggested materials: Bible and songbooks

Devotional Time Suggestions

- Song: "This Is My Father's World"

- During this time, we will look at and talk about hands – your hands and God's hands.

- First, let's talk about your hands.

  Look at your hands. The hands of every one of you have held tools with which you have worked, held children and held your Bible. Your hands are precious and may or may not be as agile as they once were, but they are still wonderfully made.

  - Psalm 139:14: "I will praise God; for I am fearfully and wonderfully made."

  Your hands can be caring, loving hands, helping hands, encouraging hands, gentle hands, unselfish giving hands, thankful hands and praying hands.

  - Psalm 24:4: "Who shall ascend to the hill of The Lord? He that has clean hands and a pure heart."

  - Job 40:14: "God established the work of your hands."

  - Ecclesiastes 9:10: "Whatsoever your hand finds to do, do it with your might."

  - Proverbs 3:27: "Withhold not good from them to whom it is due when it is in the power of thy hand to do it."

  - Isaiah 56:2: "Blessed is the man who keeps his had from evil."

- Next, let's talk about God's hands.

  - The wonderful news is that God's hands are hands on which we can depend!

- *God has loving hands.* In Nehemiah 2:8, Nehemiah wrote about "the good hand of God." John 3:16 says "God so loved the world…"

- *God has creating hands.* Isaiah 40:12: "God has measured the waters in the hollow of His hands."

- *God has powerful hands.* Daniel 11:41–42, 5:23–24: "No one can stop God's hand." Hebrews 10:31: "It is a fearful thing to fall into the hands of the living God." Philippians 4:19: "God will supply all your needs according to His riches in glory."

- *God has helpful hands.* Isaiah 59:1: "The Lord's hand is not shortened that it cannot save…"

- *God's hand can save, can help.* Psalm 92:4: "You make me glad by your deeds, O Lord, I sing for joy at the work of your hands."

- The hands of Jesus, God's Son, are saving hands. He came to earth to save us from our sins.

- When we trust God as our personal Savior; when we put ourselves into God's loving hands, we have the promise that He gives us eternal life, that He has prepared a place in heaven for us.

- Psalm 16:11: "At God's right hand, there are pleasures evermore."

- Song (with no accompaniment – many people should know it): "Put your hand in the hand of the man who stilled the water."

- Closing Prayer

If you choose to provide a craft, make a "hand" fan.

Supplies:

- Colored poster board
- Pencils
- Scissors
- Black markers
- Lace
- Glue

Cut fan shapes out of the colored poster board (make the fan large enough for a handprint). Ask each person to lay his hand on a poster board fan, and with a pencil, draw around his or her open hand on the "fan". Trace the hand drawing with a black marker. Glue lace around the edge of the fan.

Light of the World

Suggested materials: Bibles, songbooks, the words and music to the song "The Light of the World Is Jesus," different kinds of lights (candle, oil lamp, electric lamp, flashlight, lantern)

Devotional Time Suggestions

- Begin by showing and talking about the displayed lights. Ask if anyone studied by the light of an oil lamp, if anyone remembers getting electricity for the first time, if anyone was ever in a storm when the lights and electricity went out. (Allow plenty of time for people to share)

- Song: "Let the Lower Lights Be Burning"

Jesus Is the Light of the World

- In John 8:12, Jesus said, "I am the light of the world: he that follows after me shall not walk in darkness, but shall have the light of life." Jesus, God's Son, was born in a manger in Bethlehem. For 33 years, He lived on earth to bring light to the world.

- John 9:5: "As long as I am in the world, I am the light of the world."

- First John 1:5a: "God is light, and in Him is no darkness at all."

- John 12:46: "I am come a light into the world, that whosoever believeth on me should no abide in darkness."

- In Luke 19:10: Jesus said, "For the Son of man is come to seek and to save that which was lost."

- Special music (solo or a group): "The Light of the World Is Jesus"

We Are the Light of the World

- In Matthew 5:14, Jesus said "You are the light of the world; a city that is set on a hill cannot be hid. Neither do men light a candle, and put it under a bushel, but on a candlestick; and it giveth light unto all that are in the house."

- In Matthew 5:16, Jesus declared that we have a responsibility to let our love for Christ and the gospel be shown to the people around us. He admonished us to "Let your light so shine before me, that they may see your good works, and glorify your Father which is in heaven."

- Paul wrote in Ephesians 5:8 "ye were sometimes darkness, but now are ye light in the Lord: walk as children of light."

- Song: "Brighten The Corner Where You Are"

Heaven's Light

- In John 14:3, Jesus promised, "I go to prepare a place for you."

- Revelation 22:5: "there shall be no night there; and they need no candle, neither light of the sun, for the Lord giveth them light: and they shall reign forever and ever."

- We who have accepted Christ's offer of salvation have the wonderful promise of one day experiencing the light of heaven.

Song: "When We All Get To Heaven"

- Closing Prayer

If you choose to provide a craft, make a yellow sun.

Supplies:
- Dark blue paper sheets
- Bright yellow paper
- Paper word strips with the words *You are the light of the world*
- Glue
- Scissors
- Yellow crayons

Cut large round yellow circles to fit the blue paper. Glue the circle "sun" on the blue paper and glue a word strip under the yellow sun.

Trust

Suggested materials: Bible and songbooks

Devotional Time Suggestions

- Song: "'Tis So Sweet to Trust in Jesus"

- Prayer

Trust

- Without his parents' permission, a four-year-old son climbed to the top of the barn. When he looked down, he was frightened and began crying and calling for his daddy. The frantic father quickly realized that his boy could fall and be badly hurt. In a calm voice, he called up to his son "Son, jump into daddy's arms!" The child was too scared to move. "Jump son," the daddy said. "Jump and daddy will catch you. You can trust me. See, I am holding out my arms. Jump son." Trusting his dad's outstretched arms, the child jumped safely into his daddy's arms. He hugged his daddy and said "I knew you would catch me!"

Like the little boy who was in trouble and was afraid, we too have times in life when we are troubled and afraid. We have a heavenly Father whose outstretched arms are ready to give us comfort and help.

- Proverbs 3:5–6: "Trust in the Lord with all your heart, and lean not unto your own understanding. In all your ways acknowledge Him, and He will direct your paths."

- A couple was having financial difficulty and were about to lose their home. A man told them that if they gave him their mortgage payments, he could help them keep their home. The couple trusted him and gave him the money. The fellow used the money for himself and, all too late, the couple realized he had stolen their money and they lost their home. Their trust was misplaced in a smooth-talking thief.

Often, when we put their trust in people, we can be disappointed, but we can *always* put our trust in God.

- Psalm 118:8–9: "It is better to trust in the Lord than to put confidence in man. It is better to trust in the Lord than to put confidence in princes."

- Song: "Trust and Obey"

- Isaiah 26:3–4: "Thou wilt keep him in perfect peace whose mind is stayed on thee, because he trusteth in thee. Trust ye in the Lord forever, for in the Lord Jehovah is everlasting strength."

- When baby chicks are afraid, or when the nighttime comes, they rush to their mother hen. She fluffs up her wings, the baby chicks run under them, and the mother hen covers her baby chicks with her wings.

The psalmist must have had this in mind when he wrote Psalm 91:2, 4: "I will say of the Lord, He is my refuge and my fortress; my God; in Him will I trust. He shall cover You with his feathers, and under His wings shall you trust."

Psalm 57:1: "...O God, be merciful unto me: for my soul trusts in you; yea, in the shadow of your wings will I make my refuge"

- Special music (solo): "Leaning on the Everlasting Arms"

  (Ask the soloist to sing the stanzas and ask the seniors to sing along on each chorus)

If you choose to provide a craft, make a coffee filter painting.

Supplies:
- Coffee filters
- Tempera paint (slightly thinned with water) in several colors
- Paint brushes

Dip a brush in one of the paint colors and drip a little bit of paint on a coffee filter. Wait and let the paint spread. Drop paint of another color and wait. Repeat with several paint colors. Flatten the filters and let them dry.

What Do You See?

Suggested materials: Bible, songbooks, a magnifying glass and some eye glasses

Devotional Time Suggestions

- What do you see? I'm not talking about what you see with your eyes, through glasses or magnifying glasses. The question is what do you see with your heart? With your spiritual eyes?

- Many people have perfect vision in their physical eyes, but have imperfect spiritual vision.

- In 2 Kings 6:17, Elisha prayed for his servant, "O Lord, I pray thee, open his eyes that he may see."

- What do you see with your spiritual eyes?

- First, what do you see when you see yourself?

  - Do you see yourself as a wonderful person who knows you are special?

  - Do you see a person who loves himself, not with snobbish pride, but with joy because God made you and loves you?

  - Matthew 19:19a: "Thou shalt love thy neighbor as thyself." To love others, we must love ourselves.

  - Do you see yourself as a person who knows God made you and loves you, who loves God with all your heart?

  - Deuteronomy 6:5: "Thou shalt love the Lord thy God with all thy heart, and with all thy soul, and with all thy might."

  - Do you see yourself as a born-again Christian who has trusted Jesus as your Savior?

- John 3:16: "For God so loved the world that he gave His only begotten Son, that whosoever believeth in Him should not perish, but have everlasting life."

- Do you see yourself as a kind, loving and thoughtful person?

- Matthew 19:19a: "Thou shalt love thy neighbor as thyself."

- Song: "Open My Eyes"

- Second, what do you see when you see other people?

  - Do you see other people as special to God, just as you are special?

  - Do you see other people as those who need your kindness, your encouragement?

  - Ephesians 4:32: "Be kind one to another, tenderhearted, forgiving one another, even as God for Christ's sake hath forgiven you."

  - Do you see other people as needing your love and patience? I Corinthians 13 is a chapter about loving others.

  - Matthew 19:19a: "Thou shalt love thy neighbor as thyself."

  - Matthew 20:27: "Whosoever of you will be the chiefest, shall be servant of all."

  - Do you see other people as needing to know about God's love and salvation? Will you share it with them?

  - Matthew 20:28: "For even the Son of man came not to be ministered unto, but to minister, and to give His life a ransom for many."

- Third, have you been looking at yourself and at other people through someone else's eyes?

  - Looking through someone else's glasses can make you dizzy, sick and disoriented.

  - If you are looking at yourself and at other people through someone else's glasses, you cannot see well.

  - If you let other people's opinions shape your opinions, maybe you should start making your own decisions.

Proverbs 4:25: "Let thine eyes look right on, and let thine eyelids look straight before thee."

To look with your eyes is one thing.

To really see what you look at is quite another.

The see with your heart, to feel and understand, is even better.

To learn from what you understand is great, but

To act like a responsible Christian on what you learn and understand is what really matters.

- Song: "Are You Washed in the Blood?"

If you choose to provide a craft, make binoculars to share with children.

Supplies:

- Paper towel or wax paper tubes
- Glue gun
- Glue
- Contact paper with designs or wrapping paper

Cut the tube in half and glue the two halves together to make "binoculars." Cover the binoculars with contact paper or wrapping paper. Enjoy looking at each other with the binoculars. When a person is seen through the binoculars, build trust by say something kind to him or her. Give the finished binoculars to a church or civic children's group.

Worship

Suggested materials: Bible and songbooks

Devotional Time Suggestions

- Today, we are thinking about "worshiping God." The dictionary defines "worship" as "to show devotion, reverence and adoration." Worship of God includes expressing our love for God.

- Let's worship God with singing.

    Songs: "To God Be the Glory" and "All Hail the Power of Jesus Name"

- Let's worship God with prayer, telling God we love Him.

- Let's worship God with proclaiming His redemption and salvation.

    Solo: "Redeemed"

Elements in Our Worship of God

Expressing adoration and love for God

- "Thou shalt love The Lord thy God with all thy heart, and with all thy soul, and with all thy might." (Deuteronomy 6:5)

- "We love him, because He first loved us." (1 John 4:19)

Speaking praise and glory to God

- "Great is The Lord, and greatly to be praised, and His greatness is unsearchable. One generation will praise thy works to another." (Psalm 145:3–4)

- Psalm 150 is a wonderful psalm of praise. (Read the psalm or ask someone to read it)

Singing praise and glory to God

- "Praise ye the Lord, for it is good to sing praises unto our God, for it is pleasant, and praise is comely." (Psalm 147:1)

- "O God, thou God of my salvation; my tongue shall sing aloud of thy righteousness." (Psalm 51:14b)

Praying prayers of thankfulness to God

- "Be thankful unto God and bless His name. For the Lord is good; His mercy is everlasting; and His truth endureth to all generations." (Psalm 100:4–5)

- "Offer unto God thanksgiving." (Psalm 50:14)

- "O give thanks unto The Lord; for He is good, for His mercy endureth forever." (Psalm 136:1)

Praying prayers of intercession for others

- "Pray for one another" (James 5:16b)

Praying prayers of petition to God

- "The effectual prayers of a righteous man availeth much." (James 5:16c)

Preaching from God's Word

- "How beautiful are the feet of them that preach the gospel of peace, and bring good tidings of good things." (Romans 10:15)

Dedicating Ourselves to God

- "I beseech you therefore, brethren, by the mercies of God, that ye present your bodies a living sacrifice, holy, acceptable unto God, which is your reasonable service." (Romans 12:1)

- "While I live will I praise the Lord, I will sing praises unto my God while I have my being." (Psalm 146:2)

- Song, "O Worship the King"

- Close with prayer and the singing of "Doxology"

If you choose to provide a craft, make a mosaic wall decoration

Supplies:

- Twelve-inch long squares of heavy poster board
- Variety of dried beans and peas
- Glue
- Pencils

On the poster board, draw (or have the letters drawn beforehand) the letters *W-O-R-S-H-I-P*. Fill in the letter outlines with a thin layer of glue and then with beans. With a line of glue, make a design around the edges of the poster board. Allow to dry.

The Seasons

*Suggested materials: Bible, songbooks, a display of items that depict
the seasons (spring, summer, autumn and winter)*

Devotional Time Suggestions

- Begin by reading Genesis 1:1: "In the beginning, God created the heavens and the earth."

  God created a wonderful world for us to enjoy. He created the four seasons: spring, summer, autumn and winter.

  (Allow plenty of time for these discussions. Encourage participation)

- When you were kids, what are some things you and your family did in the springtime? Did any of you plant vegetable or flower gardens? Look forward to the end of the school year? Get "spring fever?" Plant crops? Did spring housecleaning?

- When you were kids, what are some things you did in the summertime? Did any of you pick cotton? Help gather crops? Cruise up and down Main Street on warm summer nights? Mow lawns? Can fruits and vegetables? Go swimming in a river, pond or pool? Have a summer job? Play baseball in the yard or the park? Go on picnics?

- When you were kids, what are some things you did in the autumn? Rake leaves? Play football or go to football games? Enjoy cookouts? Plant a fall garden? Shed your shoes? Go fishing?

- When you were kids, what are some things you did in the wintertime? Walk to school five miles in the snow? Ski? Roast marshmallows? Build a snowman? Have snowball fights? Feed the cattle in the freezing cold?

- In Psalm 1:3, the psalmist wrote about "a tree planted by the rivers of water, that bringeth forth his fruit in his season."

- God planned the earth and the seasons for our enjoyment and for us to have the food, shelter and other supplies to meet our needs. Acts 14:17b: "he (God) did good, and gave us rain from heaven, and fruitful seasons, filling our hearts with food and with gladness."

- Song: "This Is My Father's World"

- Read Ecclesiastes 3:1–8, beginning with "To every thing there is a season..."

- God knows us and knows our needs. He knows these "seasons" – the seasons that come in our lives: in our childhood, youth, young adulthood, in mid-life and in old age. He knows good times and bad times, and in the past and present, we can rely on God to guide us and help us.

- Prayer thanking God for the world He has made for us, for the seasons, for his guidance and help in every season of our lives.

- Ecclesiastes 3:11: "God has made everything beautiful in His time."

- Prayer

- Close with the song: "Savior, like a Shepherd Lead Us"

If you choose to provide a craft, make a "Thank You, God" magnet.

Supplies:
- Pastel-colored poster board cut into four-inch squares
- Colored thin-line markers
- Flower stickers
- Magnetic tape cut into three-inch strips

With the markers, decorate the squares with the words *Thank You, God* and with flower stickers. Draw a border around the square. Glue a magnetic strip on the back of the square.

The Good Shepherd

Suggested materials: Bible and songbooks

Devotional Time Suggestions

- Song: "God Will Take Care of You"

In the Psalm 23, David compares the Lord to a good shepherd.

"The Lord is my Shepherd"

- The Lord is my shepherd, your shepherd, our shepherd. Like a shepherd knows and cares for his sheep, the Lord knows and cares for you and me.

"I shall not want"

- Like a good shepherd is dependable and supplies the needs of his sheep, so we can depend on the Lord to supply our needs.

"He maketh me to lie down in green pastures"

- Like a good shepherd finds the best place for his sheep to rest in comfort of the tall green grass, so God helps us find rest. Sheep without a shepherd can't find a place to rest. Neither can we. When we follow the guidance of our Shepherd, He gives us peaceful rest.

"He leadeth me beside the still waters"

- Shepherds say that sheep tend to wander into running, rushing waters where their wool gets wet and heavy – and they drown. The shepherd leads them to still waters where they can safely drink and be refreshed. The sheep don't have to worry about where they will drink today, tomorrow and in the future. They know the shepherd will lead them. The Lord, our Shepherd will do the same for us. He will lead us to what we need. We can trust Him for today, tomorrow and in the future.

"He restoreth my soul"

- A good shepherd restores his sheep when they are hurt or frightened or lost, when they need help. Our Lord, our Good Shepherd, restores our hope, our joy, our peace of mind and our awareness that He is in charge and will help us.

"He leadeth me in the paths of righteousness for His name's sake."

- The good shepherd guides his sheep in safe paths, away from rocks, gorges and wild animals. He cares about the sheep. The Lord guides us to safe paths away from harm and evil.

"Yea, though I walk through the valley of the shadow of death, I will fear no evil: for thou art with me; thy rod and thy staff they comfort me."

- Even when leading his frightened sheep through a dangerous valley, the shepherd stills their fears, guides them with his rod and staff, keeps them safe and comforts them. The Lord, our Shepherd, faithfully guides us, protects us and does not leave us. Even in death, we can trust our Good Shepherd.

"Thou preparest a table before me in the presence of mine enemies

- God is the Shepherd who provides for us even in the face of trouble and difficulty.

"Thou anointest my head with oil"

- A good shepherd soothes his sheep with special oil that helps heal hurts and helps repel insects that harm the sheep. Our Lord will help heal our wounds and troubles. He will help keep us from harm.

"My cup runneth over"

- God fills our lives with good things. Our cups of blessings are full and overflowing.

"Surely goodness and mercy will follow me all the days of my life, and I will dwell in the house of The Lord forever."

- The love and goodness of God will be with us all of our lives. When we trust and follow our Lord, our Good Shepherd, we are assured of an eternal home with Him in heaven.

- Song: "Savior, like a Shepherd, Lead Us"

- Prayer

If you choose to provide a craft, make a sheep pin.

Supplies:

- Small sheep shapes cut out of heavy poster board
- Safety pins
- Cotton balls
- Glue

Cover the shapes with glue. Put cotton balls over the glue to make a white sheep. On the back, glue a safety pin. Allow the glue to dry.

Grade School Memories

Suggested materials: Bible, songbooks, a display of school supplies (backpack, crayons, school books, etc.)

Devotional Time Suggestions

- Back to school time! Children are back in school and already learning new things.

- Do you remember the song, "School Days?" Let's try to sing it together!

> School days, school days
> Dear old golden-rule days
> Reading and 'riting and 'rithmetic
> Taught to the tune of a hick'ry stick
> You were my queen in calico
> You were my bashful, barefoot beau
> You wrote on my slate, "I love you so"
> When we were a couple o' kids

- How many of you went to a country school? A one-room school? A town school? A city school?

- What is something good that you remember about your grade school days? Did you walk to school? Did you ride on a school bus? Did your class salute the American flag every day? Did you sing the song "America?" Did you take your lunch or buy your lunch? What did you do during recess?

- Friends were an important part of childhood school experiences. Tell us about a childhood friend.

- It's fun to remember happy school days of childhood. Do your recall a teacher's name? Teachers worked hard to help us learn. Much of what we know today is based on what we learned in childhood.

- But, learning is a lifetime task. Just because we are not in school doesn't mean that we quit learning. We must never quit learning! Senior adults can learn something new every day.

- The Bible contains some verses and thoughts about learning, and every one of them apply to us:

(Discuss each passage after it is read)

  - Deuteronomy 31:12–13: "Gather the people together, men, women, and children and thy stranger that is within thy gates, that they may hear, and that they may learn, and fear The Lord your God, and observe to do all the word of this law."

  - Proverbs 1:5: "Let the wise listen and add to their learning."

  - Proverbs 18:15: "An intelligent man is always open to new ideas. In fact, he looks for them.

  - Isaiah 1:17: "Learn to do well."

  - Matthew 11:28–29: "Come unto Me, all ye that labor and are heavy laden, and I will give you rest. Take my yoke upon you, and learn of me."

  - Philippians 4:11b: "I have learned how to get along happily whether I have much or little."

  - Second Timothy 3:14–15: "continue thou in the things which thou has learned and have been assured of, knowing of whom thou hast learned them; and that from a child thou has known the holy scriptures, which are able to make thee wise unto salvation through Christ Jesus."

If you choose to provide a craft, make a small ruler with glitter name.

Supplies:
- Six-inch long rulers
- Pencils
- Glue
- Glitter

With a pencil, print the name on the back of the ruler and outline the name with glue. Sprinkle with glitter.

God's Promises to You

Suggested materials: several Bibles, songbooks, three or four of the suggested Bible promises typed on paper strips.

Devotional Time Suggestions

Ahead of time, give the Bible promise strips to persons who can read them at the proper time during the devotional.

- Songs: "Tis So Sweet to Trust in Jesus" and "Standing on the Promises"

God's Promises

- God's promises! God always keeps his promise. He never goes back on a promise. He doesn't change His mind about a promise. Psalm 89:34: "I will not break my covenant; I will not take back one word I said."

- God's promises do not fail. Joshua 23:14: "You know with all your heart and soul that not one of all the good promises the Lord your God gave you has failed. Every promise has been fulfilled; not one has failed."

- God can do the impossible. Luke 18:27: Jesus said, "What is impossible with men is possible with God."

- God promises to forgive us. First John 1:9: "If we confess our sins, He is faithful and just to forgive us our sins and purify us from all unrighteousness."

- God promises to give us peace and rest. Isaiah 26:3: "You will keep in perfect peace him whose mind is steadfast, because he trusts in You."

- Special music: "Wonderful Peace"

- God promises to stay near us. Genesis 28:15: "I am with you and will watch over you wherever you go, and I will bring you back to this land. I will not leave until I have done what I have promised you."

- God promises to help us in time of fear and discouragement. Deuteronomy 31:8: "The Lord himself goes before you and will be with you; He will never leave you nor forsake you. Do not be afraid; do not be discouraged."

- God promises to deliver us from trouble. Psalm 50:15: "...call upon me in the day of trouble; I will deliver you, and you will honor me."

- God promises to meet our needs. Philippians 4:19: "my God will meet all your needs according to His glorious riches in Christ Jesus."

- God promises good things for you. Jeremiah 29:11: "For I know the plans I have for you, declares the Lord, plans to prosper you and not to harm you, plans to give you hope and a future."

- God promises to return. John 14:2-3: "In my Father's house are many mansions: if it were not so, I would have told you. I go to prepare a place for you. And if I go and prepare a place for you, I will come again, and receive you unto myself; that where I am, there ye may be also."

- God's promises to end death, sorrow, and pain. Revelation 21:4: "(God) will wipe away every tear from their eyes. There will be no more death or mourning or crying or pain, for the old order of things has passed away."

- Song: "Great Is Thy Faithfulness"

If you choose to provide a craft, paint plaster leaves.

Supplies (all available at hobby stores):
- Plaster-of-paris leaf shapes
- Fall-colored tempera paint
- Clear plastic spray

Paint the leaf shapes. Allow them to dry and then spray them with clear spray.

Fruit of the Spirit

*Suggested materials: Bible, songbooks, a large clear glass bowl
filled with different kinds of fruit for display*

Devotional Time Suggestions

- Prayer thanking God for the Bible and its messages to us.

- Songs: "Just a Closer Walk with Thee" and "Stand Up, Stand Up For Jesus"

Fruit of the Spirit

- Recorded in the Bible is the letter, written by the apostle Paul, to the churches at Galatia. In the letter, Paul urged the churches to be steadfast in their faith. He wrote to remind them that salvation comes only by faith in Jesus Christ. Paul reminded the Galatian church that Christian freedom does not give us an excuse to sin. Paul also reminded them that Christian freedom does not keep us from life's struggles, but that freedom will result in the "fruit of the spirit."

- In Galatians 5:22–23, Paul lists the "fruit of the spirit," which are qualities of character. When we put our faith and trust in God, we will display the "fruit of the spirit" in our lives.

  - *Love* is the first fruit of the spirit, a love that is Christ-like and unselfish. In Galatians 5:13, he wrote "by love serve one another." First Corinthians 13 describes the fruit of the spirit love.

  - *Joy* is the second fruit of the spirit – gladness of heart, rejoicing in God's love and salvation. The Spirit of God gives us joy and happiness in spite of circumstances in our lives.

  - *Peace* is the third fruit of the spirit. The Holy Spirit has peace to give us. He can give it in whatever amount we need. This peace is the inner peace that comes when a Christian puts his complete trust in God.

- *Longsuffering (or Patience)* is the fourth fruit of the spirit. This is the fruit of kindness, ready-to-help friendship – not just once, but a continuing attitude of love. It also includes a sweet disposition and showing kindness with other people, even when they try our patience.

- *Kindness* is the fifth fruit of the spirit. It includes being gracious and thoughtful of other people. A gentle spirit is one that is tenderhearted, compassionate, sympathetic and loving.

- *Goodness* is the sixth fruit of the spirit. This fruit gives us the want-to, the will to do good – doing good with kind deeds and generosity. Goodness is caring about people, people who are in need and people who need a kind word or encouragement.

- *Faithfulness* is the seventh fruit of the spirit. Faithfulness means faithful to a task, keeping promises and being dependable. It also includes being loyal and trustworthy.

- *Meekness (or Gentleness)* is the eighth fruit of the spirit. Meekness includes humility, modesty and being unpretentious. Meekness is not being a weakling. Meekness is strength under control.

- *Self-Control* is the ninth fruit of the spirit. Self-control results in temperance, sobriety, calmness, mastery of personal desires and passions. Self-discipline and disciplined behavior are significant in self-control.

- Each of these fruits of the spirit comes directly from God. However, we are responsible for doing our part. Our job is to integrate each of the fruits of the spirit into our lives.

- Song: "Trust and Obey"

- Prayer asking God for His guidance in making the fruit of the spirit a part of our lives.

If you choose to provide a craft, make slice and eat fruit slices

Supplies:
- Apples
- Oranges
- Bananas
- Paring knives
- Napkins

Carefully slice the fruit and enjoy eating it together.

Friendship

Suggested materials: Bible, songbooks, enlistment of a person who knows sign language

Devotional Time Suggestions

Songs: "Onward Christian Soldiers"

Prayer thanking God for friends and friendship.

Song: "What a Friend We Have in Jesus"

(Ask a person to do sign language while the musician plays a stanza and chorus, then ask the people to sing while the person continues to sign)

Friendship

- Friendship is important to all of us. A person who has no friends is lonely, forlorn and without companionship.

- What are some words that define "friendship?" (Loves no matter what, lifts self-esteem, has similar tastes, likes the same kinds of things, honest relationship, sympathetic, empathetic, understands, loyal, etc.)

- What are some words that describe a friend: (best friend, old friend, new friend, bosom friend, close friend, devoted friend, faithful friend, trusted friend, companion, pal, sidekick, buddy, chum, etc.)

- Proverbs 17:17 gives a good word about a friend: "A friend loveth at all times."

- Proverbs 18:24b: "A friend sticks closer than a brother." No matter what, a real friend continues to be your friend.

First Samuel contains the story of the close, loving, God-honoring friendship between David and Jonathan. Jonathan, the King's son, was a kind young man. He was a good friend to David. First Samuel 18:1 tells that "the soul of Jonathan was knit with the soul of David, and Jonathan loved him as his own soul." They make a promise to each other that whatever happened, they would always be friends.

Since Jonathan's father, King Saul, did not like David, he (David) wanted to leave the king's palace. He was afraid King Saul intended to kill him. Jonathan did not want David to leave. "My father won't hurt you," he said, but David was still afraid. He knew that he really was in great danger.

King Saul continued to hate David. He told Jonathan to kill him. But Jonathan loved David, so he made a plan. He told David "In a field not far from here, there is a great stone. Go and hide behind it. In three days, I will come with my servant and shoot three arrows by its side. If I say to my servant 'Go and find the arrows, they are on this side of you, bring them here,' then you will know that it is safe and there is no danger. But if I say to the boy, 'Look the arrows are beyond you,' then you must get away, for there is great danger."

So David hid in the field. Jonathan went to King Saul. He begged him not to kill David. King Saul did not listen. He became very angry. He threw his spear at Jonathan. Jonathan ran from the palace. With his servant, he went to the field near the great stone. Soon his arrows flew through the air. "Find the arrows," called Jonathan. "They are beyond you."

David heard. He knew Jonathan was telling him he was in danger. Jonathan's servant found the arrows and Jonathan sent him home. Then David came out of his hiding place. He put his arms around Jonathan. Jonathan told David of his father's plans to kill him and urged him to go far away where he would be safe.

First Samuel 20:42: "And Jonathan said to David, "Go in peace, forasmuch as we have sworn both of us in the name of the Lord, saying, the Lord be between me and thee and between my seed and thy seed forever." Not only did Jonathan and David honor the Lord in their friendship, but they desired that their children also be caring friends.

Friends are God-given and are to be treasured. Be sure that you are a true friend. Proverbs 27:9-10 (Living): "Friendly suggestions are as pleasant as perfume. Never abandon a friend - either yours or your father's."

- Prayer of thanksgiving for friends.

If you choose to provide a craft, write a kind note to a friend.

Supplies:

- Note paper
- Pencils
- Pens

Esther

Suggested materials: Bible, songbooks, and you may wish to assign people to read the nine parts of Esther's story.

Devotional Time Suggestions

- Songs: "Come Thou Almighty King" and "A Child of the King"

- In the Bible book of Esther, we find a story that proves Romans 8:28: "we know that all things work together for good to them that love God, to them who are the called according to His purpose."

- Special music (solo or group): "In His Time"

The Story of Esther

King Xerxes was angry because his queen disobeyed him. He banished the queen and began a search for a new queen. His empire's most beautiful young virgins were brought to the palace for a year's worth of beauty treatments so they could be presented to the king for his approval.

Esther was a beautiful young Jewish girl. Her God-given beauty caused her to be one of the young women taken to the palace. From that point on, it was a fact that Esther would either be the queen or spend the rest of her life in the king's harem.

Esther was chosen to be the queen. Mordecai, her cousin and guardian, told her not to tell anyone that she was a Jew. What neither Esther nor Mordecai realized was that God was preparing her to save her people.

Haman, the arrogant right-hand man of the king, was furious because Mordecai wouldn't bow down to honor him. Haman persuaded the king to decree that all Jews would be killed in one day – the 13th day of the 12th month. The Jews had 11 months to live.

God placed Esther in the palace for "such a time as this." Esther 4:16: Esther decided to approach the king. For a month, he hadn't asked for her. Anyone approaching him without invitation risked being killed before saying a word.

Esther had two choices. One – she could risk her life to approach the king, tell him she is Jewish and make a request to save her people. Two – as queen, she could enjoy the security of the lavish life in the palace.

Esther, putting herself in God's hands, said "if I perish, I perish," donned her queenly robes, entered the palace's inner court and stood in view of the king. She must have been greatly relieved when the king summoned her to him. She waited for God's direction. She invited the king and Haman to a banquet. At the banquet, waiting for God's timing, she invited them to a second banquet.

After the first banquet, when the arrogant Haman passed the king's gate, Mordecai again refused to bow down to him. Enraged, Haman ordered gallows built for Mordecai's hanging. Haman was horrified when he discovered that the king had chosen Haman to honor Mordecai because he had stopped an assassination attempt.

At Esther's second banquet, the timing was right for Esther to reveal that she was a Jew, beg for her life and for the lives of her people. She pointed to Haman as the one who caused the trouble. Haman begged Esther for forgiveness and accidentally fell on her. The king accused him of attacking Esther, the queen. Haman was immediately taken to be hanged. He was hanged on the gallows he had built for Mordecai.

Mordecai was given Haman's position and property. A proclamation was made for the safety of the Jews, and all enemies of the Jews were destroyed. The Jews still celebrate Purim, an annual feast to honor God for delivering the Jews from their enemies.

- Do you look to God in all circumstances of your life? Do you stand by your belief in God? Is God's perfect timing important to you? Do you celebrate the blessings you have received from God?

- Prayer

If you choose to provide a craft, make a friendship bracelet

Supplies: (available at hobby stores):
- Colored wooden beads
- Leather strips

Give each person at least four or five beads and a leather strip. As they string and tie the beads on the strips, talk about friendship.

Joy

Suggested materials: Bible and songbooks

Devotional Time Suggestions

- Begin with quoting Psalm 118:24: "This is the day which the Lord has made; we will rejoice and be glad in it." Then ask the group to quote it with you.

- Song: "O Happy Day"

Joy

- "Joy" is a happy word. One definition of "joy" is a glad feeling, happiness, great pleasure, delight.

- Let's sing a song that most of us learned in childhood. We don't need accompaniment because we know it well.

> "I have the joy, joy, joy, joy, down in my heart,
> Down in my heart, down in my heart.
> I have the joy, joy, joy, joy, down in my heart,
> Down in my heart to stay."

Sing it again, and this time, clap as we sing.

- A wonderful verse is Psalm 30:5b: "weeping may endure for a night, but joy cometh in the morning."

- Often, discouragement comes easily and we feel weary and sad. Happiness eludes us. That is the time when we need to turn to the Lord and remember all His goodness to us; all the blessings He has bestowed on us.

- Psalm 16:11: "in (God) is fullness of joy; at thy right hand there are pleasures evermore."

- When you and I are tempted to have a pity party, we need to call out to the Lord and say as David did in Psalm 51:12: "Restore unto me the joy of thy salvation." David desired to, again, feel the comfortable sense of God's saving grace. He had God's salvation, promised for the present and for eternity. David wanted his joy back. Like David, sometimes we need to renew the joy that we have in the security of God's salvation.

- Jesus said, "If you keep my commandments, ye shall abide in my love; even as I have kept My Father's commandments, and abide in his love. These things I have spoken unto you, that my joy might remain in you and that your joy might be full." (John 15:11–12)

- We must not allow Satan to steal our joy. He knows he can't steal our salvation, but he can sneak in and steal our joy.

- Nehemiah 8:10c: "the joy of The Lord is your strength." Accept this truth! With God's help, you can change from a gloomy Christian to a glowing Christian, from forlorn to cheerful, from defeated to victorious.

- Lack of joy does not honor God. Lack of joy does not show what God has done and is doing for us. Lack of joy does not show others what God can do for them.

- The Holy Spirit will help you if you call on Him to furnish the power you need to renew and maintain your joy.

- The world needs to see happy, joyful, radiant, victorious, cheerful Christians.

- Let's sing it again: "I have the joy, joy, joy, joy down in my heart"

- Prayer asking God to help us renew our joy and realize that the joy of the Lord is our strength.

If you choose to provide a craft, make poster board laced pumpkins.

Supplies:
- Pumpkin shapes cut out of orange poster board
- Hole punches
- Black or green one-fourth inch ribbon

Punch holes around the outside edge of the pumpkin shapes, lace ribbon through the holes and tie the ribbon with a bow. As the pumpkins are being laced, talk about the joy God gives us in our lives.

Be an Encourager

Suggested materials: Bible, songbooks, ten 8 1/2 x 11 posters each with one letter of the word E-N-C-O-U-R-A-G-E-R, place to display the letters as they are used in the devotional acrostic, a different person to set each letter in place at the correct time

Devotional Time Suggestions

- Today's world is a discouraging world. There is war, hate, crime, unkindness, poverty, criminal gangs and fear. But every one of us can be an encourager in this discouraging world. We can make a difference.

- Characteristics of "encourager": gives courage, hope, confidence; gives support, helps and cheers.

ENCOURAGE Is:

Every day, giving sincere encouragement to other people. Encouragement is an everyday lifestyle.

- Hebrews 3:13: "But encourage one another daily"

- Second Chronicles 32:6-7: "...and encourage them with these words: Be strong and courageous. Do not be afraid or discouraged."

Nurturing people with your sincere encouragement.

- With encouragement, Mary Kay Ash built a successful business empire. Her formula for success included telling her employees to forget their mistakes and zero in on what they do right. Give encouragement and praise, and people will do more things right and can discover abilities they never realized they had.

Comforting those who have difficulty.

- Romans 12:15: "weep with those that weep." Express comfort, but encourage joy and remembering God's blessings.

Observing and being aware of opportunities to encourage and sincerely love people.

- According to an old fable, the devil decided to have a garage sale and sell some of his well-worn tools.

- On display were some treacherous-looking instruments, including hatred, jealousy, lying and pride. Off by itself was a harmless-looking devise with a very high price tag. "What is this?" someone asked. The devil replied, "That is discouragement. It's one of my most effective tools. With it I can pry open the hearts of good servants and bring on dejection, depression and despair."

- Of course, this is not a true story. But it is true that by giving encouragement to others, you can help overcome the devil's tool of discouragement.

- First Thessalonians 5:11: "...encourage one another and build one another up"

Using scripture to encourage and help other people.

- Use John 3:16. Let's quote it together.

- Romans 15:4–5: "These things were written in the scriptures so long ago to teach us patience and to encourage us...may God who gives patience, steadiness, and encouragement help you to live in complete harmony with each other - act with the attitude of Christ toward the other."

Rejoicing with people.

- Romans 12:15b says, "weep with those that weep," but the first part of that verse is "rejoice with those that rejoice."

- For some reason, we find it easier to encourage someone who is weeping than someone who is rejoicing.

- Someone tell us about a time when you actually rejoiced and encouraged someone who was truly blessed.

Avoiding negative words; being positive.

- Job needed encouragement. His friends offered none. Job said "...miserable comforters are you all. Will your long speeches never end? What ails you...if you were in my place...my mouth would encourage you; comfort from my lips would bring you relief." (Job 16:1-5) Job's friends gave only negative words and no encouragement. Our words need to always be positive words of encouragement.

Giving encouragement and expressing Christian love and acceptance.

- When the apostle Paul and his companions were in the synagogue, the leaders said "Brothers, if you have a word of encouragement for the people, please speak." (Acts 13:15)

- People want and need our encouragement. Romans 15:1–2: "We who are strong ought to bear with the failings of the weak and not to please ourselves. Each of us should please his neighbor for his good, to build him up."

Encouraging, even when you have problems and difficulties and are hurting.

- Not only will you be helping someone else, you will be helping yourself.

- Closing song: "Brighten the Corner Where You Are"

- Prayer

If you choose to provide a craft, carve pumpkin faces.

Supplies:

- Large pumpkins for decorating the area
- Knives
- Black felt markers if you want to draw rather than cut the face on the pumpkin

Words

Suggested materials: Bible and songbooks

Devotional Time Suggestions

- In this time together, we will be thinking about our words. Do you remember the saying "Sticks and stones will break my bones, but words will never hurt me?" Do you agree with that? (Allow time for discussion)

- Song: "Wonderful Words of Life"

- We have sung about God's wonderful words to us. Now, let's talk about our words. Tell about a time when someone's words gave you joy or peace. (Allow time for responses)

- Paul, in First Thessalonians 4:16–17, described the second coming of Christ. Then in verse 18, he wrote, "Comfort one another with these words." Paul knew that good words can give comfort.

- Tell us about a time when someone's words gave you comfort. (Allow time for responses)

- A compliment or a kind word can make a difference in a person's day. Sincere, kind words can make a person feel good about himself, words such as: "You have a lovely smile," "You always look so nice," "I admire you," "I am praying for you," "I heard you singing," "You have a beautiful voice." "You are always thoughtful of others," "Thank you for all the kind things you do."

- Sometimes, we know exactly what we should say. Often, we don't give enough thought to how to say it. We sometimes speak the truth, but without love. We speak, but with such an overbearing arrogance or anger our listeners cannot hear the message; it is covered up by all the "attitude."

Obviously we need to give attention to *how* we speak, as well as *what* we speak. We need to understand what good we can do when our words are accompanied by a caring and pleasant attitude. Prov. 15:28 says, "the heart of the righteous studies how to answer, but the mouth of the wicked pours forth evil."

We are obligated to speak the truth in love, and let our speech be always with grace, "seasoned with salt, that you may know how you ought to answer each one," (Ephesians 4:15, Colossians 4:6)

- Our words should not only be caring and pleasant, but should also be honest and true. When and if we make a promise, when we say we will take a responsibility, when we agree to do something for someone, we must be trustworthy.

First John 2:4–5 speaks to our being trustworthy. "He that says, I know (God), and keepeth not his commandments, is a liar, and the truth is not in him. But, whoso keepeth his word, in him verily is the love of God perfected."

- Song: "O How I Love Jesus"

- Proverbs 25:11: "A word fitly spoken is like apples of gold in pictures of silver."

This verse is a beautiful picture – apples of gold, surrounded by or set in silver. A similar statement is in Proverbs 16:24: "Pleasant words are like a honeycomb, sweetness to the soul and health to the bones."

- A "word fitly spoken" would be the right thing, said at the right time, in the right place, to the right person, in the right way and for the right purpose.

- Special music (solo): "I Love to Tell the Story"

- Close with the Bible verse Psalm 19:14: "Let the words of my mouth and the meditation of my heart be acceptable in thy sight, O Lord, my strength, and my redeemer.

If you choose to provide a craft, make golden apples.

Supplies:

- Small plaster-of-paris apples from a hobby shop or small red apples from a dollar store (one apple for each person)

- Gold tempera paint

- 1/2 inch wide brushes

- Clean spray paint

Allow each person to paint and completely cover his apple with gold paint, and, when the paint is dry, spray the gold apple with the clear spray paint. As they paint, remind the senior of the Bible verse "A word fitly spoken is like apples of gold in pictures of silver."

Eagles

*Suggested materials: Bible, songbooks, a large picture of an
eagle and/or large eagle figurines for display*

Devotional Time Suggestions

- Songs: "The Old Rugged Cross" and "The Solid Rock"

- Isaiah 40:31: "They that wait upon the Lord shall renew their strength; they shall mount up with wings as eagles; they shall run, and not be weary; and they shall walk, and not faint."

- Eagles are strong.

  - They are one of the strongest of all the birds. They are hard workers who need their strength. They build strong nests, some of which are 30 to 60 feet above the ground. Their nests can be about seven feet high and five and a half feet across the top. The larger nests consist of about two wagon loads of materials. Eagles have great strength which they have to maintain.

  - When he wrote Isaiah 40:31, Isaiah must have been thinking about the strong, bold eagle. The verse begins, "those who wait on the Lord shall renew their strength." Our strength is in the talents and abilities that the Lord given us. Our strength is in spiritual strength.

- Eagles have strong, wide wings.

  - Some weigh as much as 15 pounds and have a wing span of more than eight feet. Using their strong wings, they fly high, swiftly and gracefully. With their strength, they can spread their wings and glide smoothly, high above the ground, for hours at a time.

  - Isaiah 40:31 says that, like the eagle, we can mount up with wings. Of course, not literal wings, but with renewed strength, we can keep on doing what the Lord has for us to do, whatever it is. None of us can say "I can't do anything."

Our task may be praying, witnessing and displaying Christian attitudes using our various talents. And, like the eagle smoothly gliding through the air, we can feel the freedom and joy of using what strength we have to serve the Lord.

- Eagles are not afraid.

  - They do what they have to do without fear and are willing to rely on their strength to defend themselves, their young and each other from predators.

  - Like the eagle, we need not be afraid, but can rely on the Lord, our strength and our redeemer. John 14:27: "Peace I leave with you, my peace I give unto you: not as the world gives, give I unto you. Let not your heart be troubled, neither let it be afraid."

  - We are told that when a storm is approaching, the eagle flies to a high place and waits for the winds. When the storm hits, the eagle spreads its wings so that the wind will pick it up and lift it above the storm. The eagle doesn't escape the storm, but uses the storm to lift it up.

  - When in our lives, there are storms of sickness, tragedy, disappointment and failure, God's power can help us soar above the storms. God can and will guide us through the storms of life.

- Eagles are protectors.

  - When a storm threatens the eaglets in the nest, the adult stands in the nest, faces the wind and rain and spreads its wings half-open to make a wonderful, warm shelter for the protection of the eaglets huddled beneath the wings.

  - We can be protectors when the storms of evil threaten our children, our families and our nation. We can provide the warm shelter of prayer, of sharing God's Word, of using whatever tools we possess. The good news is that we can depend on God for protection. Psalm 36:7: "How excellent is Thy loving kindness, O God! Therefore the children of men put their trust under the shadow of Your wings."

- Special music (solo): "Under His Wings"

- Reread Isaiah 40:31 and pray, thanking God for the promises He give us in His Word.

If you choose to provide a craft, make picture soap.

Supplies:

- Small bars of soap
- Small photographs or small magazine pictures that fit on the soap
- Glue
- Brushes

Brush glue on the top side of the soap and place the picture on the glue and then brush glue on top of the picture. When the glue dries thoroughly, the soap should be ready to use. (If desired, for the top coat, melted wax can be used instead of glue)

Habakkuk

Suggested materials: Bible and songbooks

Devotional Time Suggestions

- Song: "To God Be the Glory"

- Sentence prayers by three assigned people.

- Habakkuk was a prophet who loved and trusted God. He cared about his people – God's chosen people, who were quarreling among themselves. They were snarling and devouring each other; they were oppressive and unjust. Habakkuk was a man of clear faith and personal closeness to God. He searched diligently for truth and went to God for answers. It was the responsibility of Habakkuk to carry God's message to the people.

Habakkuk's Contrasts of the Faithful and the Faithless
Habakkuk 2:4-5, 1:11, 2:8

The faithful live with integrity. The evil nature of the faithless is destructive.

Success vs. Failure

Failure: a wicked soul, inevitable failure and destruction. (v. 5): "…never satisfied, always grasping"

Success: satisfied, knowing and obeying God and experiencing His care. (v. 2:4): "the just shall live by faith" Success – even when life seems difficult.

- Song: "Great Is Thy Faithfulness"

Peace vs. Turmoil

Turmoil: constantly, greedily trying to get more and more in order to find satisfaction which never comes. (v. 5)

Peace: God-given peace in the midst of trouble. Knowing that God is in control and can and will, in His own time, make things happen. And, in the meantime, God can and will give us peace and comfort.

Faithful Service vs. Living Death

Living Death: Godless, completely living without hope, unfulfilled. (v. 2:4-5)

Faithful Service: Understanding and knowing God's love and faithfulness. Faithfully serving God – not just once in awhile, not just when things go badly and we need help, but every day, in whatever circumstances we find ourselves.

Stability vs. Instability

Instability: betrayed by his own wickedness, arrogance, drunkenness. Always needy for another drink, another drug, more money, more power. (v. 2:4-5)

Stability: living with complete trust in God, even if God's people have forgotten God's ways; even if there is illness, loneliness, and even in the face of trouble.

Justified and Forgive vs. Guilty and Unforgiven

Guilty and Unforgiven (v. 2:4, 1:11): "their guilt is deep; they claim their power is from their gods. They are totally without faith and trust in the one true God. How awful it must be not to have the assurance of God's love and forgiveness."

Justified and Forgiven (v. 2:4): "the just shall live by faith." What a magnificent feeling to know that by trusting God as personal Savior, He saves us and keeps us saved for eternity. We must take God's message to those who are unsaved.

Happiness and Future vs. Joyless Woe and Doom

Joyless Woe and Doom: how sad and hopeless it is when a person dies without having trusted the Lord as personal Savior...with no hope of heaven and eternal life with God.

Happiness and Future Life: peace, comfort, joy in the knowledge that, in trusting Jesus as personal Savior, you have the promise and hope of eternal life in heaven with God.

- Song: "When We All Get to Heaven"

- In spite of difficulty and the wickedness of God's people, the prophet Habakkuk bravely delivered God's message.

If you choose to provide a craft, make Thanksgiving cards.

Supplies:

- Colored 8½ by 11-inch paper sheets
- Small Thanksgiving-themed cookie cutters (turkeys, leaves, pumpkins, etc.)
- Pencils
- Colored thin-line felt markers
- Envelopes

Fold the paper sheet in half, and then in half again. Set a cookie cutter on the paper and draw around it. With the markers, color the shapes – make any designs or lines desired. Print or write a message. Put the finished card in an envelope.

Thanksgiving

Suggested materials: Bible, songbooks, fall decorations including fall leaves and fruit

Devotional Time Suggestions

- It's Thanksgiving time!

- Prayer asking God to help us, during this time, to count our blessings and be thankful.

Thanksgiving

God is good to give us so many blessings. Name some of the blessings God has given you. (Allow time for the group to think about and name blessings)

- Song: "Count Your Blessings"

- Scripture – Psalm 50:14a: "Offer unto God thanksgiving"

- Prayer, thanking God for the blessings that have been mentioned.

God is good to allow us to live in this wonderful country. Name some of the blessings of being an American. (Allow time for response)

- Song: "America The Beautiful"

- Scripture – Psalm 100:4-5: "Enter into his gates with thanksgiving, and into His courts with praise: be thankful unto Him, and bless His name. For the Lord is good; His mercy is everlasting; and his truth endures to all generations."

- Prayer, thanking God for America and for our freedoms.

God is good to send His Son, Jesus to die for our sins.

- Song: "Jesus Paid It All"

- Scripture – 2 Corinthians 9:15: "Thanks be to God for His unspeakable gift."

- Prayer thanking God for His love and His sending Jesus so that we can have eternal life.

God is good to give us the Bible, His Holy Word.

- Song: "Break Thou The Bread of Life"

- Scripture – 2 Corinthians 2:14: "Thanks be to God for through what Christ has done, He has triumphed over us so that now wherever we go He uses us to tell others about the Lord and to spread the gospel like a sweet perfume."

- Prayer thanking God for His Word and for the comfort and guidance it gives us.

God is good to give us the opportunity to go directly to Him in prayer.

- Song: "Sweet Hour of Prayer"

- Scripture – Philippians 4:6: "Don't worry about anything; instead, pray about everything; tell God you needs, and don't forget to thank Him for His answers."

- Prayer thanking God for being able to go to Him in prayer.

God is good to give all His blessings to us.

- Song: "Blessed Be the Name"

- Scripture – James 1:17: "Every good gift and every perfect gift is from above, and cometh down from The Father."

- Prayer, thanking God for His wonderful gifts.

God is good to give us victory now and eternally.

- Song: "Victory In Jesus"

- Scripture – 1 Corinthians 15:57: "thanks be to God, which giveth us the victory through our Lord Jesus Christ."

- Prayer, thanking God for giving us victory in Jesus.

In you choose to provide a craft, make waxed leaves.

Supplies:

- Variety (color and sizes) of leaves
- Wax paper
- Iron
- Old newspapers

Cover an ironing board or other surface with several heavy layers of newspapers. Place a sheet of wax paper on the newspapers and arrange several leaves on the wax paper. Put another sheet of wax paper over the leaves. With a medium-hot iron, press a leaf at a time between the wax paper sheets. Hold the iron in place for thirty seconds. Press all the areas of the wax paper. Lift off the wax paper and remove the leaves. They should be waxed enough to keep their shape. The leaves can be used in centerpieces or by themselves.

Prayer

Suggested materials: Bible, songbooks, words and music to the song
"Take Your Burden to the Lord and Leave It There"

Devotional Time Suggestions

God created you and me in His image. God created us to have emotions – emotions and the longing to be loved are legitimate. The emotions we all feel at times of fear, joy, heartache, sadness, loneliness and despair. All emotions we can share with our heavenly Father. God made us, and He understands our needs.

Prayer

- God gives us the gift of prayer, of talking to Him, of telling Him our feelings and our needs, of "taking our burdens to the Lord and leaving them there."

- Special music (solo or singing group): "Take Your Burden to the Lord and Leave It There"

- We can take any problem, need, emotion and difficulty to God in prayer. We can share any joy and happiness with God in prayer. In prayer, we have and build a personal relationship with our God, our Maker, our Savior.

- I Thessalonians 5:16 admonishes us to "pray without ceasing." When a teenage daughter asked her daddy what that meant, he answered that it means we should stay close to the Lord and stay on praying ground!

- Prayer is not just for calling on God when we are in trouble, but prayer is an everyday relationship with God.

- Personal prayer can be anytime, anywhere.

- Matthew 6:6–8 describes a special time of personal prayer: "When thou prayest, enter into thy closet, and when thou has shut the door, pray to thy Father which is in secret; and thy Father which seeth in secret shall reward thee openly. But when ye pray, use not vain repetitions, as the heathen do: for they think that they shall be heard for their much speaking. Be not therefore like unto them: for your Father knoweth what things ye have need of before you ask Him."

- The psalmist speaks about personal prayer in Psalm 34:4: "I sought the Lord, and He heard me."

- Song: "I Need Thee Every Hour"

- Read Luke 11:9–13. In this passage, Jesus talked about praying and asking and God's answering.

- James 5:16 reminds us to "pray for one another."

- Jesus also talked about people praying together. In Matthew 18:19–20, Jesus said, "That if two of you shall agree on earth as touching anything that they shall ask, it shall be done for them of my Father which is in heaven."

- Not only should we pray for our loved ones, friends and others, but Jesus mentioned another aspect of prayer again in Matthew 5:44. He said "love your enemies" and "pray for them which despitefully use you and persecute you."

- Jesus gave us a model prayer. We call it "The Lord's Prayer." He said, "After this manner therefore pray ye."

- Let's close by saying "The Lord's Prayer" together.

If you choose to do a craft, make a Thanksgiving tree.

Supplies:

- Large piece of poster board on which is drawn a tree trunk and branches
- Various leaf-color construction paper sheets
- Scissors
- Glue

Ask each person to cut our several different shaped leaves. On each leaf, have them write one thing for which they are thankful. Glue the thank you leaves to the tree branches.

The Annunciation of Mary

Suggested materials: Bible, songbooks and some simple Christmas decorations to begin the Christmas season

Devotional Time Suggestions

- We are beginning a wonderful season of the year – the season when we celebrate the birth of Jesus Christ.

- Christmas Carol: "Away in a Manger"

The Angel Gabriel Appears to Zacharias

In this devotional time, we will begin with the account of the angel Gabriel's speaking to Zacharias in the temple. (Luke 1-11-13)

Zacharias and his wife, Elizabeth, were "well stricken in years." They had no children because Elizabeth "was barren." The angel, Gabriel, appeared to Zacharias and told him that he and Elizabeth "shall bear a son, and thou shalt call his name John. Gabriel described John as filled with the spirit of God.

John, called John the Baptist, was to preach repentance and faith in God. He was "to make ready a people prepared for the Lord." John said, "he that cometh after me is mightier than I, whose shoes I am not worthy to bear." (Matthew 5:11)

- Christmas Carol: "O Little Town of Bethlehem"

The Angel Gabriel Appears to Mary

God sent the angel Gabriel to the city of Nazareth where he spoke to an innocent, young Jewish woman. She was espoused (what we would call engaged) to a man named Joseph, who was a descendant of David. The young virgin's name was Mary.

Gabriel came to her and said "Hail, thou that are highly favored, the Lord is with thee: blessed are thou among women." (Luke 1:28)

Mary was startled and wondered what this salutation meant.

Gabriel said, "Mary, don't be afraid. You have found favor with God. You will conceive in your womb, and bring forth a son, and shall call His name Jesus. He will be great, and will be called the Son of the Highest: and the Lord God will give unto Him the throne of his father David. And he will reign over the house of Jacob forever; and of his kingdom there will be no end." (Luke 1:31-33)

Mary asked, "How is that possible? I have not been with a man."

Gabriel told her "The Holy Spirit shall come upon you, and the power of the Highest shall overshadow you; therefore also that holy thing which shall be born of you shall be called the Son of God." (Luke 1:35)

Gabriel told Mary that her cousin, Elizabeth, was pregnant, even though she had been unable to have a child.

Then Gabriel made a fantastic statement: "For with God nothing shall be impossible."

Mary accepted. She said "be it unto me according to thy word." (Luke 1:38)

Mary accepted her role as mother to God's Son and changed the world forever.

Mary's "yes" was obedient and willing to do God's will.

Mary said yes to the angel Gabriel. She became the mother of the Savior of the world. The birth of God's Son is what we should celebrate every day, especially in December.

- Prayer thanking God for Mary's acceptance of God's will, asking God to bless this holiday season's celebration of Jesus' birth, and asking God's help in our acceptance of His will for our lives.

- Christmas Carol: "Joy To The World"

If you choose to provide a craft, make clay angels.

Supplies:
- White craft clay (homemade or from craft store)
- Clear acrylic spray

Make an angel by shaping a ball of clay for the body, connecting a smaller clay ball for the head. Form two wing shapes and attach one to each side of the body. Allow the "angels" to dry. Spray with clear acrylic spray.

The Shepherds

Suggested materials: Bible, songbooks and a manger scene with shepherd figures included

Devotional Time Suggestions

- Christmastime is a delightful season of the year. It is during this time we celebrate the birth of God's Son, Jesus.

- Christmas Carols: "Silent Night" and "Hark, The Herald Angels Sing"

The angels appeared to shepherds.

We just sang about the angels signaling the birth of Jesus. It is interesting that God did not send the angels to main town Bethlehem. He sent the angels out to the countryside where shepherds were watching their sheep.

Of all the people who could have traveled to the animal barn where Jesus was born, God chose shepherds to be the first to worship Jesus. God didn't send just one angel. He sent a whole host of angels to announce Jesus' birth. The fact that they appeared to shepherds is proof that Jesus came to seek and to save lost people, no matter what their station in life, whether it is lowly or high and noble.

The shepherds were poor.

They were sheep herders, field laborers who were protecting the sheep from harm. The angels could have been sent to shopkeepers or merchants, but the angels took their message to poor shepherds who were out under the night sky. The angels did not take their message to rich people in their fine homes.

The shepherds were not socially acceptable.

They were not the type of people who were invited to important social events. They probably knew little about polite society. They did not sit in places of government. Yet, the angels brought their message to the hillside where the shepherds were doing their job, seeing that the sheep did not wander, get lost or get attacked by fierce animals. God didn't send the angels to give the message to kings and men of social class, but rather to lowly shepherds.

The shepherds were not scholars.

They were not necessarily ignorant. They were wise in the care of sheep; however, they were very likely not well-educated scholars. But God didn't choose to send the angels to scholars. He did not send angels to the school room or to the law office full of books or to the king's palace. He sent them to the shepherds.

The shepherds were not religious leaders.

They were not the religious leaders of the day, not the rabbis, not the priests in the temple. They probably couldn't even read the temple scrolls. But that didn't matter; God sent the angels with His good news to shepherds in the hills outside Bethlehem.

The shepherds responded to the angels' message.

Even though they were startled and afraid when the angels appeared to them, the shepherds believed the message. They knew the message was a special message about a special event. They hurried to the animal barn to see the newborn baby, God's Son, in the manger. They bowed down and worshiped Him, the newborn King, born of a virgin and sent by God "to seek and to save that which was lost." (Luke 19:10)

The shepherds shared the Good News that the angels told them.

They told everyone they saw "they made known abroad" the news of the angels' message and the baby in the manger. God's offer of His Son isn't only to the shepherds. He sent it to the shepherds to be shared with the world.

- Song: "Joy To The World"

- Read Luke 2:7-17 and pray, asking God's blessing on the reading of this wonderful story and thanking for sending His Son and for the shepherds who shared the message which God sent for all of us.

If you choose to provide a craft, make "shepherd's crook" candy sticks.

Supplies:

- Clear-wrapped peppermint sticks shaped with a crook at the top, resembling a shepherd's crook

- Holiday ribbon that is easy to tie "Merry Christmas" Christmas stickers or other stickers that depict Christ's birth

Tie a generous amount of ribbon on the candy sticks, and then stick Christmas stickers on each end of the ribbon.

Celebrating the Christmas Story

Suggested materials: three Bibles, songbooks and Christmas decorations, including a manger scene

Devotional Time Suggestions

- Begin with singing, with or without accompaniment, some popular songs such as 'Jingle Bells," "White Christmas," or "Sleigh Bells Ring."

- Read the Christmas story from Luke 2:7–19.

  (If possible, ask three people to read Luke 2:7–19, each taking turns reading a verse, starting with verse 7)

- Prayer thanking God for Jesus, for the wonder of His miraculous birth and for the saving power of Jesus our Savior.

Singing Christmas Carols

(If you choose to do so, intermingle solos and/or the singing of a special group in with the singing of the carols)

- "It Came upon a Midnight Clear"
- "Silent Night"
- "O Little Town of Bethlehem"
- "Away in a Manger"
- "Hark, the Herald Angels Sing"
- "O Come, All Ye Faithful"
- "Joy to the World

- Christmas is a wonderful time of year. As often as you have opportunity, share the Christmas story with friends, loved ones and other folks you meet. God bless each of you during this season.

- Prayer thanking God for the Christmas story, for sending His Son, Jesus, to be born in a manger, to save us from our sins and give us eternal life.

If you choose to provide a craft, make Christmas mobiles.

Supplies:

- Wire hangers (a local cleaners is a good source)
- Gold cord or Christmas ribbon
- Colorful Christmas balls

Using different lengths of the cord or ribbon, tie at least three (five is a better number) Christmas balls to each hanger, making sure that the balls are tied securely. The top of the hanger can be carefully twisted so that the mobile can be hung almost anywhere.

Gifts

Suggested materials: Bible, songbooks and several empty boxes wrapped like gifts

Devotional Time Suggestions
Gifts wrapped in pretty packages

- Let's talk about gifts. Gifts are wonderful! What gifts have you received during the holiday season?

- Think for a moment and then be ready to tell us about the best gift you ever received for Christmas or birthday or some other special occasion. (allow time for responses) Isn't it fun to get gifts?

God's Gifts to Us

- Besides gifts wrapped in pretty packages, we often take for granted some of the wonderful gifts that God has given us. Name some of them. (allow time for responses)

- James 1:17: "Every good gift and every perfect gift from God is from above, and comes down from the Father."

God's Most Important Gift to Us

- The most important and wonderful gift from God is His promise of eternal life. We all love John 3:16. Let's quote it together. God's promise of eternal life never grows old.

- Romans 3:23: "For the wages of sin is death, but the gift of God is eternal life through Jesus Christ our Lord."

- Ephesians 2:9–10: "For by grace are you saved through faith; and that not of yourselves: it is a gift of God. Not of works, lest any man should boast."

God's Gifts of Talents and Abilities

- God gives each of us different gifts of talents and abilities. 1 Corinthians 7:7b: "Every (person) has his proper gift of God, one after this manner and another after that. Each of us has different abilities and talents. The important thing is that we use our gifts to honor the Lord.

- Paul wrote to Timothy "Neglect not the gift that is in you." His words can apply to us as well. We must not neglect to use the gifts that God has given us.

Thank God for the gifts He has given us. Ask four people to pray prayers of thanks to God:

1. For family and friends who love us and give us gifts
2. For God's wonderful gift of eternal life when we trust Him as Savior
3. For the different gifts and talents that you have given each of us
4. That we will each use our talents and gifts, large and small

- As you leave this devotional time, remember that a smile, a kind hello and kind words can be your gifts to the people you meet, to your family and to your friends.

If you choose to include a craft, make paper snowflakes.

Supplies:
- White tissue paper cut into squares
- Scissors

Fold a square of tissue paper into quarters, and then fold in a triangle shape. Cut small shapes along the folded edges, and then unfold it to see a snowflake. Every person's snowflake will be different. Talk about the fact that God makes every snowflake with a beautifully different shape. Tape the snowflakes on windows and glass doors.

SUGGESTIONS FOR FOUR "FIFTH WEEK" DEVOTIONAL TIMES

1. Who Is My Neighbor

- Suggested songs:

    - "Open My Eyes That I May See"

    - "Brighten the Corner Where You Are"

    - "Trust and Obey"

- Ask, "Do you have or have you had a favorite neighbor? Why was he or she your favorite? Allow time for responses.

- Bible passage: Matthew 22:37–39: "...Love thy neighbor as thyself..."

- Luke 10:30–37 contains the answer Jesus gave to the man who asked, "Who is my neighbor?"

- Prayer for our neighbors and friends, asking God's help in becoming more aware of opportunities to minister to other people.

2. Wise and Foolish

- Suggested songs:

    - "Are You Washed in the Blood?"

    - "I Know Whom I Have Believed"

    - "Stand Up, Stand Up for Jesus"

- The parable of the wise and foolish virgins (Matthew 25:1–10)

- What is the basic difference in the wise and foolish virgins?

- The parable of the wise and foolish house builders (Matthew 7:24–27)

- What is the difference in the two builders?

- Prayer thanking God for His wisdom and guidance.

3. A Love Story

- Suggested songs:

  - "Love Divine"

  - "Love Lifted Me"

- The beautiful love story of Ruth and Boaz (Ruth, Chapters 2–4)

  Compare their story to God's love for us.

- Special music (solo): "The Love of God"

- Prayer thanking God for His great love for us.

4. Making Melody

Suggested songs:

  - "He Keeps Me Singing"

  - "In My Heart There Rings a Melody"

- Scriptures:

  - Ephesians 5:19–20: "…singing and making melody in your heart to the Lord."

  - 1 Chronicles 16:9: "Sing unto (God), sing psalms unto Him and talk of all His wondrous works."

  - 1 Chronicles 16:23: "Sing unto the Lord, all the earth; show forth from day to day His salvation."

  - Psalm 81:1: "Sing aloud unto God our strength: make a joyful noise unto the God of Jacob."

  - Psalm 101:1: "I will sing of mercy and judgment: unto You, O Lord, will I sing."

- Talk about the God-given joy of praising the Lord with songs and singing.

- Song: "Joy to the World"

- Prayer thanking God for the joy of singing His praises.

ABOUT THE AUTHOR

Willa Ruth Garlow is a writer and motivational speaker who lives in Oklahoma City. She has authored materials for Lifeway Christian Resources, Nashville, Tennessee and for other magazines and periodicals.

She has been a keynote speaker or seminar leader in 34 states, in Europe, Asia, Africa and South America. For two summers, Willa Ruth and her husband, J. Lyle, taught at The Baptist Seminary in Budapest, Hungary.

Mrs. Garlow graduated from Oklahoma Baptist University and attended Southwestern Seminary in Fort Worth, Texas. She was presented Oklahoma Baptist University's Outstanding Alumni Achievement Award. She was awarded the Distinguished Service Award by the faculty of Educational Ministries at Southwestern Seminary in Fort Worth, Texas.

Willa Ruth considers her most important roles to be wife, mother to Dawnellen and Sam, grandmother to five, and great grandmother to nine!